Globalization

THE INTERNATIONAL INSTITUTE FOR RESEARCH
AND EDUCATION (IIRE)

Series Editor: PETER DRUCKER

Other titles available

Fatherland or Mother Earth?
Essays on the National Question
Michael Löwy

Understanding the Nazi Genocide
Marxism After Auschwitz
Enzo Traverso

Globalization
Neoliberal Challenge, Radical Responses

Robert Went

Translated by Peter Drucker

Foreword by Tony Smith

Pluto Press

LONDON • STERLING, VIRGINIA
with

The International Institute for Research and Education (IIRE)

First published 2000 by Pluto Press
345 Archway Road, London N6 5AA
and 22883 Quicksilver Drive, Sterling,
VA 20166-2012, USA

www.plutobooks.com

British Library Cataloguing in Publication Data
A catalogue record for this book is available from
the British Library.

ISBN 0 7453 1427 9 hbk
ISBN 0 7453 1422 8 pbk

Library of Congress Cataloging-in-Publication Data
A catalog record for this book has been applied for.

Designed and produced for Pluto Press by Chase Publishing Services
Typeset from disk by Gawcott Typesetting Services
Printed in the European Union by Antony Rowe Ltd, Eastbourne, England

Contents

List of Figures and Tables

Figures

Tables

IIRE Notebooks for Study and Research

Thousands, even millions of social activists, in trade unions, NGOs, ecological movements, students' and women's organisations, are wrestling with questions about a changing, globalizing world. What ended and what began in history when the Berlin Wall fell? What realistic models can we put forward now in opposition to the reigning neoliberalism? How can we resist neoliberalism's lurking counterparts: nationalism, racism, fundamentalism, communalism?

The International Institute for Research and Education shares these grassroots activists' values: their conviction that societies can and must be changed, democratically, from below, by those who suffer from injustice, on the basis of wide-ranging international solidarity. We exist to help progressives pose the questions and find the answers that they need.

Since 1982 we have welcomed hundreds of participants from over 40 countries to our courses and seminars. Our Ernest Mandel Study Centre, opened in 1995, hosts lectures and conferences on economic and social issues of the post-Cold War world. We have built a network of Fellows who help with these tasks. Our Amsterdam headquarters and library are a resource for researchers and for gatherings of socially-minded non-profit groups.

Since 1986 the results of our work – on economic globalization, twentieth-century history, ecology, feminism, ethnicity, racism, radical movement strategy and other topics – have been made available to a larger public through our monograph series, the Notebooks for Study and Research. The Notebooks are now published in English as books by Pluto Press. Past Notebooks have also been published in other languages, including Arabic, Dutch, French, German, Japanese, Korean, Portuguese, Russian, Spanish, Swedish and Turkish. Back issues of the 20 pre-Pluto Press Notebooks are still available directly from the IIRE.

For information about our publications and other activities, please write to us: IIRE, Postbus 53290, 1007 RG Amsterdam, Netherlands; email: iire@antenna.nl. Donations to support our work are tax-deductible in several European countries as well as the US.

Foreword

'Globalization' remains one of the most contested concepts of our day. There has long been a need for a clear survey of recent developments in the global economy and the most significant interpretations of these changes. With Robert Went's Notebook, this need has now been superbly met. But Went goes far beyond a mere survey of facts and opinions. Building upon the work of Ernest Mandel and others, he reveals how the leading theoretical accounts of globalization are profoundly flawed. He also shows how the practical conclusions derived from these flawed accounts fails to address the interests of the vast majority of the world's population. Most importantly, he outlines how a more adequate account can contribute to social struggles for a quite different form of globalization from what we see today.

It is impossible to reflect the comprehensiveness of Went's overview of the globalization debate here. In order to simplify matters I shall refer to some implications of Went's research for the assessment of certain neoliberal and progressive perspectives.

Most mainstream theorists and policy makers accept one or another variant of the neoliberal view of globalization. From this perspective it is natural and rational for capital to flow from developed economies, where there are ample funds for investment but an aging population, to 'emerging' economies, with a relatively youthful population and a great need for investment capital. Economic growth in emerging economies then supposedly leads to a global convergence in living standards, while returns on investments flow back to developed economies, allowing their pensioners to retire in comfort.

In recent years these allegedly beneficial capital flows have been interrupted by severe financial crises in the emerging economies. In the neoliberal account the blame for these crises falls primarily on governments. Government officials in emerging economies established a system of 'crony capitalism' connecting the state, banks, and corporations in personal (often familial) networks. Excessive levels of debt, speculation, and outright corruption were hidden by substandard accounting practices. When the depths of these problems became clear, who could blame international investors for withdrawing their capital?

Of course one could ask why such investments had been made in the first place, given the fact that 'crony capitalism' was hardly a secret. Here neoliberals place much of the blame on the governments of the developed world. When investors are reasonably confident of being bailed out by these governments and the international agencies they influence, they have every incentive to pursue high returns in emerging markets, despite all the risks.

Given this theoretical perspective, a number of policy proposals follow at once. Crony capitalism must be dismantled. High accounting standards must be imposed throughout the global economy. Bail outs of investors must be limited to exceptional cases involving systematic risk to the global economy as a whole. If these and similar measures are implemented, neoliberals assert, the 'natural' and 'rational' flows of capital will automatically follow, bringing a global rise of prosperity in its wake.

The corruption of political and economic elites must indeed be condemned. Accounting transparency should be encouraged as well (although all dimensions of corporate activity should be open to public inspection, not just those of interest to investors). And providing public subsidies to wealthy investors is indeed perverse. Nonetheless, the neoliberal account has astonishingly little connection to social reality. Robert Went documents in great detail how the 'natural' flow of capital in the global economy leads to uneven development and radical inequalities, not a convergence of living standards. Units of capitals at the centre of the global system are able to reproduce and expand their advantages over regions at the periphery in a number of ways. Investment capital from dominant regions flows mostly to other dominant regions. The direct investment that does go to the periphery is mostly used to purchase existing assets, resulting in a reverse flow of wealth from the poorest regions of the world to the centres of capital accumulation. Many other mechanisms further this reverse flow, including the extension and enforcement of intellectual property rights, inducements to capital flight, never-ending debt crises, and the structural adjustment programmes that shape economies in the periphery to the needs of 'first world' capital. Went's monograph establishes beyond a shadow of a doubt that neoliberal proposals are really attempts to rationalise the process whereby circuits of capital from the leading regions are able to appropriate surplus value produced throughout the global economy.

Went also explains clearly why these attempts at reform are doomed to fail on their own terms: they are attempts to rationalise a system with an irredeemable element of irrationality at its heart. Financial speculation and instability are endemic to global capitalism. The greatest threat of systematic crises in the global economy today surely lies with the excessive debt levels, trade imbalances, currency speculation, and insane stock market valuations found in the regions at the centre of the capitalist system, not with the 'crony capitalism' of the so-called developing world, as horrible as that might be.

Various progressive social movements call for reforms of global capitalism to alleviate the problems neoliberals ignore and worsen. Stagnant real wages limit effective demand for commodities. Global poverty leads to uncontrolled migration, terrorism, criminal activity, and epidemics. The present path of capitalist development generates long-term environmental harm. These and other potentially catastrophic difficulties cannot be cordoned off to the poorer regions of the world. Sooner or later they affect the well-being of the wealthy as well. Avoiding these so-called 'global public bads' is thus in the long-term interests of just about everyone. There is a practical imperative to develop a 'global civic society' with strong non-governmental organisations capable of educating the general public and lobbying effectively for appropriate legislation. Just as neoliberals struggle for 'best practice' global accounting standards, progressives must struggle for 'best practice' global standards regarding labour rights, work conditions, environmental practices, and so on. Corporations that fail to adhere to these obligations should forfeit their right to participate in the global economy. If such a regime of global governance were instituted, many progressives conclude, the global capitalist economy could then function in a fair and efficient manner.

Reforms are certainly possible in capitalism, including reforms that profoundly improve the lives of working men and women and their communities. But Robert Went provides powerful reasons to be sceptical of the claim that 'global public bads' can be adequately overcome in the capitalist global order, even in principle. Capitalism rests upon a fundamental asymmetry of power between capital and labour; if the power of labour gets too strong, the 'rules of the game' allow those who own and control capital to institute vicious counter-attacks. Capitalism also necessarily involves the concentration and capitalisation of capital; Went documents how a relative handful of corporations have amassed unprecedented concentrations of economic and political power. As we have already noted, capitalism also includes a host of mechanisms that necessarily lead to profoundly uneven development in the global economy. Finally, whatever reforms are won in the course of progressive social struggles are subject to serious attack when a 'long wave' of declining profitability commences, as it inevitably must.

In brief, all reforms are necessarily partial and precarious as long as the 'rules of the game' that define capitalism are in place. As long as capitalism persists the vast majority of the world's population in both the centre and the periphery will be threatened by increasing inequality, economic insecurity, and erosion of the material conditions necessary for happiness and autonomy.

The conclusion to be drawn from this is not to withdraw from struggles for progressive reforms. We must instead attempt to formulate and implement policies that are intelligible and attractive to all those harmed by global capitalism, yet which have a dynamic leading to an ever-more profound questioning of the capitalist order. In the book that follows Robert Went provides a powerful argument for such policies and in the final pages he outlines some crucial examples. Anyone wishing to understand why radical social change is necessary in our 'age of globalization' ought to study his immensely important contribution closely.

Tony Smith

Acknowledgements

This book would never have been written without the inspiring and thought-provoking comments, suggestions, doubts and criticisms of Gilbert Achcar, Daniel Bensaïd, Hans Boot, Peter Drucker, Maxime Durand, Gisela Dütting, Ewald Engelen, Rob Gerretsen, Elsa van der Heiden, Anke Hintjens, Michel Husson, Joost Kircz, Francisco Louçã, Jos Oostveen, Henk Overbeek, Rienke Schutte, Jan-Willem Stutje, Michel Tilanus, Charles-André Udry, Marcel van der Linden, the participants in the August 1994 Amsterdam NGO Summer School, the participants in the September 1994 IIRE European Youth School, and above all Geert Reuten. Thanks to Peter Drucker for his painstaking translation into English and useful suggestions for updating the book.

Unfortunately Ernest Mandel, from whom I learned so much over the past 20 years, died before the text was finished, so I have had to do without his inspiring comments and suggestions.

List of Abbreviations

APEC	Asia-Pacific Economic Cooperation (17 countries including the US and Japan)
BIS	Bank for International Settlements
EU	European Union
FDI	Foreign direct investment
G7	Canada, France, Germany, Italy, Japan, the UK and US
GATT	General Agreement on Tariffs and Trade
GDP	Gross Domestic Product
GNP	Gross National Product
IMF	International Monetary Fund
MERCOSUR	Southern Cone Market (Argentina, Brazil, Paraguay and Uruguay)
NAFTA	North American Free Trade Agreement (Canada, Mexico and the US)
NGOs	Non-Governmental Organisations
NICs	New Industrialising Countries
OECD	Organisation for Economic Cooperation and Development (organisation of the world's richest countries)
OTC	'Over-the-counter' derivatives
TNC	Transnational corporation
UNCTAD	United Nations Conference on Trade and Development
UNDP	United Nations Development Programme
VVD	People's Party for Freedom and Democracy (Dutch right-wing party)
WTO	World Trade Organisation

Introduction

> I used to think if there was reincarnation I wanted to come
> back as the president or the pope or a .400 baseball hitter.
> But now I want to come back as the bond market. You can
> intimidate everybody.
>> James Carville, Clinton's 1992 campaign manager[1]

> As recently as five years ago it would have been unimagin-
> able that thousands of people would fill the streets and
> hundreds of people getting arrested over trade and capital
> flows … The WTO architects probably didn't have this in
> mind when they designed it, but maybe we should give
> thanks for their work.
>> Doug Henwood, economist[2]

> [T]hough the facts may be on the side of the free traders,
> though global trade really ought to have mass public
> support, one can hardly deny that the opponents are
> winning the propaganda war.

Economist Paul Krugman, seen by many as a future Nobel
Prize winner, strikes a sombre note over crumbling public
support for international trade and capital flows: globalization
is 'tolerated', he says, 'but it is not loved'.[3] He is not the only
one. Preparing for the World Trade Organisation (WTO)
conference in Seattle at the end of 1999, the chief US nego-
tiator warned that the 'single greatest threat to the multilateral
trade system is the absence of public support'.[4]

After the WTO summit's failure, *Business Week* urged its
readers to take the 50,000 demonstrators in Seattle seriously.
Globalization does not have positive results for everyone, it
conceded, and a 'backlash' is looming.[5] Its headline over the

results of a US opinion poll – 'A Survey of Discontent' – was no exaggeration. Over half of those surveyed agreed that business has too much power and influence in the US, and three-quarters agreed that the benefits of the 'new economy' are being unevenly divided. Most surprising, a majority expressed sympathy for the protesters during the 'battle of Seattle'.[6] Anxious commentators and editorialists in the business press around the world warned policymakers that they must preach the gospel of free trade to the people before the tide of public opinion turns even more against globalization.[7]

Yet no one can claim that the public has not been told about economic globalization. On the contrary, it is almost impossible nowadays to open a newspaper or magazine without being treated to an article that deals with it in one way or another: the hunt for big money in internationalised, deregulated capital markets; the growing international division of labour inside multinational corporations; increasing worldwide competition for markets and market niches; or the global players' strategies, acquisitions and endless restructurings.

If so much has already been written about globalization, why add one more book to the pile? Because so much is wrong with the way in which globalization and the factors behind it are usually written about; and because the way in which globalization is used to legitimate or push through government policies is open to so many criticisms. The concept is abused in at least three different ways.

To begin with, the way in which capital markets, multinationals and international organisations such as the IMF, World Bank, WTO, OECD and G7 function restricts governments' policymaking abilities.[8] University of Leuven Professor Ricardo Petrella sums up the reigning economic logic in six commandments, which are increasingly replacing the biblical ten:

> Thou shalt globalise. Thou shalt incessantly strive for technological innovation. Thou shalt drive thy competitors out of business, since otherwise they'll do it to you. Thou shalt liberalise thy national market. Thou shalt not countenance state intervention in economic life. Thou shalt privatise.[9]

Governments that fail to play by these rules are denied access to capital or have to pay punitively high interest rates.

The general manager of the Bank for International Settlements (BIS) stated in his bank's 1994 annual report that the benefits of free movement of capital are beyond question. This is the most productive way to allocate financial resources, and 'the discipline that is thereby imposed on governments is by and large healthy'.[10] Pundits dismiss the idea that the financial markets are undermining democracy by asserting that the decisions made by millions of investors and lenders are themselves inherently democratic; or that voters will make more responsible decisions with markets to guide them; or simply that markets know better than citizens.

Whatever the rationale that may be given, countries that try to protect their markets, companies or traditional sectors risk international sanctions. Countries that fail to satisfy multinationals' demands are in grave danger of seeing production move elsewhere or investments take flight. Increased concentration of capital has put excessive, in fact uncontrollable power in the hands of a small group. A few hundred of the world's largest industrial firms control trillions of dollars worth of productive activity. These companies' veto can be enough to hold up all sorts of important political decisions. Financial markets have become the world economy's judge, jury and policeman.[11]

Second, politicians of various stripes are eager to point to the increasingly internationalised economy in order to justify harsh, unsaleable and unpopular policies. For example, governments all over Europe have justified one round of austerity policies after another by appealing to the Maastricht Treaty's convergence criteria, which countries had to meet in order to qualify for the single European currency that is supposed to strengthen Europe's competitive position on the world market. They forgot too easily that they were the ones who drafted, approved and promulgated the Maastricht Treaty in the first place. The same holds true for the Stability Pact, which determines that the countries taking part in the Monetary Union must all bring their budgets 'close to balance'. Globalization becomes in this way an alibi for lack of political imagination, cowardice, social anorexia and anti-social policies.

Finally, the growing interpenetration of the world's economies is used to justify turning over more and more power, influence and authority to international organisations and structures such as the EU, NAFTA, the WTO and the UN. As a result the roles and options available to national parliaments and governments are being steadily constricted. The underlying idea is that,

> because of fundamental changes in the international institutional environment, the laws of the market have inevitably and increasingly undermined the possibilities for independent economic and social policies. It follows from this statement that these international, institutional rules must be adapted in accordance with World Order principles in order to abolish, or at least limit, the dictatorship of blind market laws without eliminating the positive effects of the market, such as efficiency in production and marketing and technological advances.[12]

Even if there is far more talk about international coordination than there is coordination in practice, the rhetoric is becoming louder and louder.[13] The tendency towards globalization is being used as an excuse to give unaccountable, bureaucratic international organisations more and more authority to decide and punish, and increasingly to limit the scope for economic or social choices at the national and regional levels, by means of international treaties, rules and structures.

This book looks at the underlying driving forces behind increasing economic globalization, and the dynamics and consequences of a more and more internationalised world economy.

Chapter 1 gives a number of facts about globalization. Capitalism has always been an international system. But if we examine contemporary financial and trade flows and changes in corporate organisation, we see that new qualitative developments have occurred since the 1980s. A section on 'the down side of globalization' uncovers the fact that these changes are having major consequences. It is followed by a section which untangles the reality of globalization from its ideologies and myths.

How can the tendency towards globalization be explained? As a rule, globalization is portrayed as an unavoidable and irreversible process, which is rolling over us like some major natural phenomenon and drastically reshaping our lives. According to this approach, globalization arises from new technological developments. Revolutions in telecommunications and data processing, for example, make it possible to move capital in a fraction of a second of 'real time' from one end of the world to the other, and enable 'captains of industry' to run corporate activities spread around the world minute by minute from their headquarters. Chapter 2 weighs this technological-determinist explanation and finds it wanting. Technological possibilities play an important role in globalization, but technology by itself does not change the world. That only happens when institutional, economic, social, legal and other barriers to new applications are cleared out of the way. Political decisions and changes in social relationships of forces are prerequisites for this.

In the following chapters we ask what made possible the radical political, social, economic and institutional changes that cleared the way for the process of globalization. We outline and analyse the postwar development of capitalism with the help of Marxist long-wave theory. After first giving a picture of the development of this theory at the beginning of Chapter 3, we describe and explain how the postwar expansive period (the 'Golden Age' up until the mid-1970s) originated and came to an end. Then in Chapter 4 we analyse how capitalism has developed since the economic watershed of 1974–75. The processes of restructuring set in motion in the early 1980s have led to enormous social, cultural, economic, political and institutional changes, and the tendency towards globalization has played an important role in this.

Chapter 5 concludes this study with a glance at the future. Following from the analysis of the earlier chapters, its first conclusion is that there can be no going back to the specific postwar period of expansion. Continuing globalization – for the time being the most probable outcome – will lead to a more and more pervasive dictatorship of the market; to greater social inequality as the result of a dual polarisation process, both within countries and on a world scale among different countries; to progressive levelling down of wages, working conditions and social security; to extensive migratory flows; to life-threatening ecological deterioration and destruction; to a greater role for unaccountable international institutions and regional entities; and to further whittling-away of democracy. But major international crises cannot be ruled out, because major risks are associated with the globalization process. The problem is that there is virtually no international regulation or control to speak of that could replace the national control and regulatory mechanisms that have succumbed to deregulation, privatisation and financial innovations. The Mexican crisis at the end of 1994 and the crisis that broke out in mid-1997 in Asia show how unstable and unpredictable the globalised world economy has become.

But a positive way out of the deadly, contemporary economic and social dynamic is also conceivable. Such a positive alternative requires putting in question globalization and free trade as well as the dictatorship of the market. Never before has there been such a gap between what is possible and what is actually happening. A drastic redistribution and democratisation of means, resources and structures still offers us a world to win. In place of the widespread idea that society can no longer be changed, left organisations, the trade union movement and other social movements must find ways to restore hope and rebuild a credible, social, ecological, feminist and internationalist alternative. This is no simple task, but it is a necessary one. This book is meant to make a modest contribution to the urgent work of puncturing the myths of the reigning economic orthodoxy and putting new ideological weapons in the hands of organisations and movements that want change.

CHAPTER 1

Globalization: What's New about It?

Gone is the dream of the leisure society, along with that of full employment, that of a regular, secure job and that of a compassionate society. Is there an end to this? And where does barbarism begin?

Manfred Bienefeld[1]

In corporate headquarters' corridors these days, they say that the only way to really insult an entrepreneur is by wishing him luck in creating a lot of jobs ... Modern entrepreneurs think globally. From this standpoint, the nagging unions who say that higher profits should mean more jobs in your own country sound provincial.

Jos Teunissen and Cees Veltman[2]

In the literature on globalization one can schematically distingish three different opinions. For authors such as former US Secretary of Labour Robert Reich and the Japanese business guru Ohmae, globalization is a definite trend that is changing everything and against which national states or trade unions can do very little or even nothing.[3] Partially in reaction, writers such as Ellen Meiksins Wood ('The concept of globalization as it is commonly used is the heaviest ideological albatross around the neck of the left today'[4]) and David Gordon strongly question the importance, newness and effects of globalization. Among other things, these authors stress that companies are not really 'footloose' – free to move whenever and wherever they choose around the world – or say that the world economy was at least as internationalised at the end of the nineteenth century as it is today.

The 'g-word' has been given many different meanings, they say, and has become ideology.[5]

Between these two extremes is a third position that can be summed up in the proposition that *globalization is an exaggeration*. Authors who subscribe to this position acknowledge that there are significant changes under way with important implications for the organisation and functioning of the world economy. But they explain at the same time that we are (still?) far from a truly globalised economy, that there are no linear developments and that many of the claims of globalization ideologues are untenable.[6] This book can be situated within this current.

It is true that many ideologues, employers and politicians exaggerate the extent and effects of globalization. Many poor policy decisions are being justified with facile, inaccurate assertions about globalization, which is portrayed as a quasi-natural phenomenon to which we have no choice but to adapt ourselves. But neither fact should make us close our eyes to real, qualitative changes in the functioning and organisation of the world economy. Four aspects of globalization are of particular interest.

First, we are seeing an increase in the number of truly integrated global markets. For production, capital flows and trade, the world economy is increasingly one, and national markets are being replaced by global markets. Global markets are becoming the natural strategic horizon for major corporations, investors and speculators.[7] It should not be forgotten that, not only in absolute figures but also as a relative share of the world population, more people are working today under capitalist relations than ever before in history.[8] This is the result of changes that have come quickly. 'In little more than a decade most of the non-OECD world, comprising four-fifths of the world's population, has moved to privatize, liberalize and deregulate, and is moving to compete actively on world markets.'[9]

Second, the weight of multinationals continues to grow. Globalised companies are emerging that try to plan and organise the conception, production and distribution of their products not only regionally, but also globally, with major consequences for these companies' structure. No multinational is really footloose; studies that show this are a useful antidote to the simplistic, fashionable claim by globalization ideologues that companies can move their activities instantly to other parts of the world. But there are limits to the insights afforded by this type of qualification:

> [S]ome researchers have recently been able to show that the usual indices of multinationalisation (percentage of activity abroad, number of subsidiaries, etc.) of conglomerates do not show a break during the 1980s. This is the case for countries such as the US or UK, clearly less so for other countries (France for example). But in any event this misses the essential point: the qualitative mutations that occurred in the conglomerates' structure, their internal and external organisation, and the origin of their revenues. As early as the late 1980s J. Dunning was able to lay out clearly the characteristics of what he called 'the new type of multinational'.[10]

Third, we are seeing an increase in problems of governance or regulation on a global level. This is a result of the fact that national states are becoming – making themselves – less effective, while the construction, reinforcement and legitimacy of supranational institutions, which are playing an increasing role, are lagging behind the development of the global economy. We are seeing a complicated, risky process of shifts in power and responsibilities among various levels of regulation, in which supranational 'unelected world governments' (the G7, IMF, WTO, BIS, OECD, etc.) and regional blocs (the EU, NAFTA, MERCOSUR, etc.) are getting to play a greater role while national states are still the most important entities.

Fourth and most obviously: if there is one thing that has globalised since the early 1980s, it is macroeconomic policies. Since the counterrevolution that took place in economics at the end of the 1970s, the monetarist and neoclassical paradigms have become unchallenged in official institutions and the political mainstream. Organisations like the IMF, the

World Bank and WTO are applying variants of the same neoliberal prescriptions everywhere in the world.[11] Austerity programmes in the OECD countries, shock therapy for the former bureaucratically planned economies and structural adjustment programmes for Third World countries all have the same characteristics – export-oriented growth, more market and less state social policy, free trade, deregulation, labour market flexibility, privatisation, priority to the holy war against inflation ('price stability') – while full employment is no longer a policy goal.[12]

Looking at the facts in more detail makes clear just how extensive the changes under way are. Some of these changes do not in themselves have major effects, or are not historically unprecedented.[13] But the combination and scope of these factors are new, and are changing the way in which the world economy functions.

Trade

Since the end of the Second World War, international trade has been growing steadily: from $60 billion in 1948, $110 billion in 1958, $240 billion in 1968, $900 billion in 1978, to more than $2 trillion in 1988. It has increased more quickly than either production or domestic trade. Taking account of inflation and taking 1963 as our base year (=100), by 1993 total world production rose to 223, while total export volume rose to 314. Since the late 1980s international trade has been growing twice as fast as the world's combined gross national products. At least a third of international trade takes place inside multinationals, which does not in itself detract from the fact.

This is not the first time that international trade has increased. Figure 1.1 shows that from 1870 to 1913 the world economy became steadily more open. The following years put an end to the trend, but from the late 1940s on, the world economy once more became steadily more open. Only in 1968 did it reach the level of 1913.

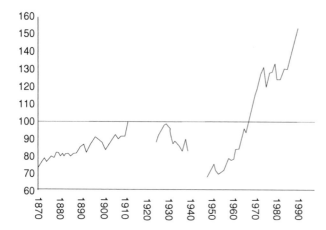

Figure 1.1 Index of trade orientation (openness) of the world economy (1870-1990)[14]

Note: An increase in this index indicates that the world economy is becoming more open; a decline indicates that the world economy is becoming more closed.

In discussions about whether globalization is really a new phenomenon, comparisons with the period 1870–1913 play an important role, since at that time too there was a considerable increase in international trade and a growing openness of the world economy. Based on data for trade flows (Table 1.1), some have concluded that the world economy today is hardly more open than it was in 1913.[15]

Table 1.1 Exports and imports of goods as a percentage of gross domestic product in current market prices

	1913	1950	1973	1994
France	30.9	21.4	29.2	34.2
Germany	36.1	20.1	35.3	39.3
United Kingdom	47.2	37.1	37.6	41.8
Netherlands	100.0	70.9	74.8	89.2
United States	11.2	6.9	10.8	17.8
Japan	30.1	16.4	18.2	14.6
Arithmetical average[16]	42.6	28.8	34.3	39.5

But this argument has been criticised, on various grounds. One objection is that trade figures should be modified to take account of changes that have taken place over the years in the structure of economies. Today, for example, the service sector is much bigger than it was in 1913. Because services are largely nontradeable, one can assume that trade as a percentage of GDP has declined due to that fact alone.[17] Trade figures also hide important changes in the nature of the goods being traded. In 1913 most traded goods were raw materials, while today most are (parts of) industrial products.

Moreover, trade figures do not show important qualitative changes. Because of the existence of regional blocs, many trade-replacing investments are being made. Japanese investments in the US and the EU fall into this category: Japanese multinationals sell 95 per cent of the products they produce in the US and the EU in those same markets.[18]

In the end everyone seems to agree that world trade has reached an unprecedented level. The discussion is mainly about *when* the pre-First World War level was matched and overtaken. On balance, the conclusion seems justified that we are seeing today 'the widest-ranging trade liberalization the world has ever witnessed'.[19]

International mergers and takeovers

There is a sharp increase in international mergers and takeovers and direct foreign investment – an annual increase four times greater than the annual growth rate of international trade.[20] The liberalisation of capital movements accelerated considerably in the 1980s, and today hardly any country in the Western world sets limits to international capital flows. According to the BIS, the volume of transnational investment since 1980 has increased more than 20 times.[21]

Foreign direct investments (FDI) have grown immensely. According to UNCTAD, 'during the past decade and a half, global integration seems to have proceeded faster through FDI than through trade'. By 1997 at least 143 countries and territories had adopted special laws to encourage foreign investment, and most countries have adapted their economies in some way or another in order to attract foreign investors. It is no wonder that FDI flows at the end of the 1990s are nearly twice what they were a decade earlier, and seven times as high as in 1980. World FDI stock – 'the capital base for TNC operations' according to UNCTAD – increased by 10 per cent in 1997 alone, to an estimated $3.5 trillion.[22]

International ownership of assets has increased thanks particularly to lower transaction costs, liberalisation, deregulation and the key fact that far more assets are traded than in the past. In the years before the First World War relatively few assets were traded – there were only 300 different shares on the New York stock exchange in 1910, for example. Today, as a consequence of the growth of trade in derivatives, that number has grown immensely.

Financial globalization

While foreign direct investment has been increasing, it is still marginal compared with short-term movements of capital, which have grown explosively. Capital is flying all over the world and is extremely sensitive to exchange and interest rates. In 1971, just before the Bretton Woods system of stable exchange rates collapsed, over 90 per cent of exchange transactions in the world bore some relation to financing trade or future investment, while less than 10 per cent was speculative. Today these figures are reversed: over 90 per cent of all transactions are speculative.[23]

Financial globalization and the corresponding increase in speculation have been spectacular. In 1990, for example, daily turnover on international currency exchanges amounted to $500 billion. By 1994 the turnover on these exchanges reached an average of $1200 billion a day, and by 1998 $1500 billion a day.[24]

> Twenty-four hours a day, trillions of dollars flow through the world's major foreign-exchange markets as bits of data traveling at split-second speed. No more than 10 percent of this staggering sum has anything to do with trade in goods and services. International traffic in money has become an

end in itself, a highly profitable game. John Maynard Keynes, who had intimations of how technology might one day be harnessed in the service of nonrecreational gambling, predicted the rise of this 'casino economy' as he called it. Yet as banking activities have become more global and more speculative, the credit needs of billions of people and millions of small businesses are not met.[26]

Table 1.2 World exports per year and daily turnover on currency markets (in billions of dollars)[25]

Year	(A) Daily turnover on currency markets	(B) World exports per year	B/A
1979	75	1546	20.6
1984	150	1800	12.0
1986	300	1998	6.7
1990	500	3429	6.9
1994	1200	4269	3.6

In the early 1970s the central banks in the rich industrialised countries had reserves eight times greater than the average daily turnover on currency markets. In 1995, with $640 billion in their vaults, they had only about half of the daily turnover. This means that central banks can do little, either independent or jointly, to counter coordinated attacks in the markets against particular currencies.[27]

The financial markets are doubtless the most globalised markets. While it was still possible 20 years ago – or a few years more or less depending on the country – to speak of national financial markets, since then they have been increasingly integrated. Deregulation and financial innovations – in 1980 financial futures, swaps and options still hardly existed – have contributed to a great extent to these developments. Important as they are, the foreign exchange markets

are only one of the foundations of financial globalisation. They were the first pillar of it, but they are not the only pillar and today they are doubtless not the most important. From the point of view of how the capitalist system in its contemporary form functions, they are less important than the liberalised, deregulated bond markets on which Treasury bonds and other forms of public debt are traded, or than stock markets.[28]

The market in financial derivatives – which in many countries until recently was simply considered gambling – has also mushroomed. Federal Reserve Chairman Alan Greenspan has called the extraordinary development and expansion of financial derivatives 'the most significant event in finance during the past decade'.[29] Most of them are unregulated 'over-the-counter' (OTC) derivatives. In June 1998 the BIS estimated the aggregate value of OTC derivatives worldwide at $70 trillion; by March 1999 Greenspan said the figure had to be closer to $80 trillion.

OTC derivative trading involves enormous risks for the stability of the international financial system, as the near-collapse of the hedge fund Long-Term Capital Management made clear in 1998. Brokers oppose regulation of this trading because of the tremendous profits to be made from it, and central banks generally yield to the brokers' pressure. If big financial institutions threaten to go under in a panic, taxpayers will have to pay the bill. Institutions that are 'too big to fall' are always bailed out. Profits are privatised, losses are socialised.

These changes in the financial sector also have negative effects on productive sector investment and job growth. Among the major consequences of the 'financialisation' of the world economy are: short-term thinking on the financial markets; macroeconomic instability because of increasing financial volatility; and a policy bias towards protecting the value of financial assets rather than expanding output.[30] The financial sector, controlled by banks and other financial institutions, functions today in large part independently of the real economy.

Technology

The extremely rapid development and spread of new technologies plays a major role in all this. Between 1975 and 1986 global production of technology multiplied six times, while international trade in high-tech products multiplied nine times.[31] Economists have distinguished three different processes that are often lumped together in discussions as 'technoglobalization', pointing out that the degree of internationalisation varies widely among the three. Globalization is most advanced in the process of *exploiting* new inventions: in OECD countries in the 1980s applications of patent rights in countries other than the country where the patent was granted went up by an average of 6 per cent each year. International technological *cooperation* (through either technological cooperation among different companies or joint authorship of scientific papers) also rose by an average of 6 per cent each year in 1985–89 by comparison with the years 1980–84.

Genuinely international *production* of new technology grew far more slowly, by contrast. Multinationals remain far more dependent for their research and development activities on their national states' facilities and infrastructure than is often claimed.[32] There is considerable evidence that 'national innovation networks' are still playing a dominant role in technological development and innovation.

More and more companies are taking advantage of new technologies and drastically reduced transport and telecommunication costs to produce their goods and services, at least in part, through production processes spread around the world. In 1956 it was possible for 89 telephone conversations to take place simultaneously through the undersea telephone cable between Europe and North America. Today the daily peak in simultaneous trans-Atlantic conversations by means of satellites and fibre optics is roughly a million. International telephone connections have become simpler, more accessible and cheaper, and faxes, spoken words and computer-generated data can reach every corner of the planet in a few moments. A growing number of people and companies find it easier and easier to meet, travel, send goods, receive images, exchange images, cooperate and compete across frontiers.

'The global assembly line'

Products from cigarettes to cars are assembled today with parts brought together from every corner of the world.

The headquarters of running shoe producer Nike is located in Beaverton, Oregon, for example. Most of its 9000 employees work in management, administration, laboratories or logistics. None is involved in production. That is subcontracted to independent companies in Korea, Taiwan (the two countries where the most advanced models are made), Thailand, Indonesia and China. These in turn subcontract production of components and other necessary material to still other local companies. All told Nike provides work in this way to 75,000 employees.[33]

This development has major consequences for how labour is organised and for employees' positions in multinationals. If the company thinks it profitable, it can close or move its operations; more often it can threaten to do so in order to extract concessions from trade unions. Threats to move major manufacturing plants may be empty given the costs and disadvantages involved, but can nonetheless be effective in extracting concessions. The World Health Organisation and International Labour Organisation have pointed out a further consequence of this globalization: 'The continuing shift of industrial production to low-cost sites in developing countries where worker protection is lower is likely to increase the global incidence of occupational disease and injury.'[34]

Law firms, insurance companies and data entry companies are also increasingly organised as a 'global assembly line'.[35] Swissair lowered its wage costs by 8 million Swiss francs by moving part of its administration to Bombay, where 'you can hire three Indians for the cost of one Swiss'. Improvements in computers, software, modems and communications systems make spreading work around the world increasingly easy and attractive. US factories were shifting work abroad in the 1960s and 1970s too, but the difference is that today an increasing part of these moves is happening electronically, which means that they occur more quickly, more easily and at a lower cost. An employer who has no expensive factories or other 'sunk costs' to write off can shift work more quickly from one spot to another when another location proves cheaper.

Multinationals

The number of enterprises operating transnationally is growing by leaps and bounds. In 1997, according to UNCTAD, there were 53,000 such companies with at least 448,000 foreign affiliates. The value of international production attributed to multinationals was $3.5 trillion as measured by accumulated stock of Foreign Direct Investment and $9.5 trillion as measured by estimated global sales of foreign affiliates. Multinationals' share of the world economy continues to grow. The ratio of foreign direct investment to global GDP is now 21 per cent; foreign affiliate exports are one-third of world exports; and GDP attributed to foreign affiliates accounts for 7 per cent of global GDP.[36]

The size of the largest multinationals gives them considerable power. The world economy is led by a few hundred giant multinationals, which are often larger than sovereign nations (see Table 1.3).

Table 1.3 The world's top 100 economies, 1998[37] (corporations in italics)

	Country/corporation	GNP/Sales ($ million)
1	United States	7,922,651
2	Japan	4,089,910
3	Germany	2,122,673
4	France	1,466,014
5	United Kingdom	1,263,777
6	Italy	1,166,178
7	China	928,950
8	Brazil	758,043
9	Canada	612,332
10	Spain	553,690
11	India	421,259
12	Netherlands	388,682
13	Mexico	380,917
14	Australia	380,625
15	Republic of Korea	369,890
16	Russian Federation	337,914
17	Argentina	324,084
18	Switzerland	284,808
19	Belgium	259,045

	Country/corporation	GNP/Sales ($ million)
20	Sweden	226,861
21	Austria	217,163
22	Turkey	200,505
23	Denmark	176,374
24	*General Motors*	*161,315*
25	Hong Kong	158,286
26	*DaimlerChrysler*	*154,615*
27	Norway	152,082
28	Poland	150,798
29	*Ford*	*144,416*
30	*Wal-Mart*	*139,208*
31	Indonesia	138,501
32	Thailand	134,433
33	Finland	124,293
34	Greece	122,880
35	South Africa	119,001
36	Iran	109,645
37	*Mitsui*	*109,373*
38	*Itochu*	*108,749*
39	*Mitsubishi*	*107,184*
40	Portugal	106,376
41	Colombia	106,090
42	*Exxon*	*100,697*
43	*General Electric*	*100,469*
45	*Toyota*	*99,740*
46	Israel	95,179
47	Singapore	95,095
48	*Royal Dutch/Shell*	*93,692*
49	*Marubeni*	*93,569*
50	*Sumitomo*	*89,021*
51	*IBM*	*81,667*
52	Venezuela	81,347
53	Malaysia	79,848
54	Egypt	79,208
55	Philippines	78,896
56	*AXA*	*78,729*
57	*Citigroup*	*76,431*
58	*Volkswagen*	*76,307*
59	*Nippon T & T*	*76,119*
60	Chile	71,294
61	*BP Amoco*	*68,304*
62	*Nissho Iwai*	*67,742*
63	Ireland	67,491

	Country/corporation	GNP/Sales ($ million)
64	*Nippon Life*	*66,300*
65	*Siemens*	*66,038*
66	*Allianz*	*64,875*
67	Pakistan	63,159
68	*Hitachi*	*62,410*
69	Peru	61,079
70	*US Postal Service*	*60,072*
71	*Matsushita Electric*	*59,771*
72	*Philip Morris*	*57,813*
73	*Ing Group*	*56,469*
74	*Boeing*	*56,154*
75	New Zealand	55,787
76	*AT&T*	*53,588*
77	*Sony*	*53,157*
78	*Metro*	*52,126*
79	Czech Republic	51,843
80	*Nissan*	*51,478*
81	*Fiat*	*50,999*
82	*Bank of America*	*50,777*
83	*Nestlé*	*49,504*
84	*Crédit Suisse*	*49,143*
85	*Honda*	*48,748*
86	United Arab Emirates	48,666
87	*Assicurazioni Generali*	*48,478*
88	*Mobil*	*47,678*
89	*Hewlett-Packard*	*47,061*
90	Algeria	46,461
91	Hungary	45,623
92	*Deutsche Bank*	*45,165*
93	*Unilever*	*44,908*
94	*State Farm Insurance*	*44,621*
95	*Dai-ichi Mutual Life*	*44,486*
96	Bangladesh	43,970
97	*Veba Group*	*43,408*
98	*Hsbc Holdings*	*43,338*
99	*Fortis*	*43,200*
100	Ukraine	42,731

According to the World Bank,

> TNCs control 70 per cent of world trade ... [A]lmost all
> primary commodities are each now marketed by fewer than
> six multi-commodity traders ... The top five companies

have 77 per cent of world cereal trade; the biggest three companies in bananas have 80 per cent of world banana trade; the biggest three cocoa companies have 83 per cent of world cocoa trade; the biggest three companies have 85 per cent of tea trade; and the biggest four companies have 87 per cent of world trade in tobacco.[38]

The 200 largest multinationals control half of the global trade in goods. They are concentrated especially in the more dynamic sectors of the world economy, particularly in electronics, chemicals, automobiles, drugs and machinery.[39]

In the past multinationals invested in other countries in order to be able to produce and sell their goods in markets protected by import restrictions. With the fall of tariff barriers, as governments around the world opened their frontiers for goods and capital flows, there has been a qualitative change in the nature of multinational investments. There is now 'a far greater degree of geographical and organizational integration of production and the emergence of an *integrated international production system*', in the words of an UNCTAD report. Multinationals have shifted from a 'stand alone strategy' to a 'simple integration strategy', and now they are increasingly headed towards a 'complex integration strategy', in which they transform their geographically dispersed affiliates and fragmented production systems into 'regionally or globally integrated production and distribution networks'. In the process 'they introduce significantly new characteristics into the process of international economic integration'.[40]

Regional blocs

There have been so many initiatives for establishing free-trade zones, customs unions and common markets that they are almost impossible to keep track of. The long-established EU, NAFTA (the US, Mexico and Canada) and APEC (17 Asian and Pacific Rim countries, including the US and Japan) are the best known, but international agreements have been multiplying rapidly in recent years in every part of the world. According to the WTO, 109 regional agreements were reported to GATT between 1948 and the end of 1994; almost a third of them were signed between 1990 and 1994.[41] The UN Economic Commission for Latin America and the Caribbean counted over 30 multilateral and bilateral treaties and subregional pacts in its part of the world alone.

Alongside these agreements, the long-awaited GATT treaty was finally concluded in 1994, leading to sweeping liberalisation of international trade. This process falls under the strict supervision of the WTO, which began its activities on 1 January 1995 in Geneva. While GATT and the OECD portrayed the treaty as a 'win-win game', many Third World countries had their legitimate and very serious doubts. The way that rich countries brushed aside the Third World's concerns in the last phase of the GATT negotiations only reinforced their reservations. Luis Fernando Jaramillo, chairperson of the G-77 group of Third World countries during the GATT talks, said afterwards: 'Despite insisting that the negotiations were global in character, the countries of the North refused in the end to accept any discussions, even bilaterally, with the countries of the Third World.' The new GATT treaty and WTO

> will increase the global deregulation of commerce in goods and open it in agricultural products and services, as well as further facilitating transnational investment and the formation of global financial markets. It will increase the power of transnational capital and the transnational corporations (TNCs) ... and further remove both from national controls. This, in turn, will intensify the destructive competitive clash of these economic titans and the nations that fight to play host to them.[42]

What's new: summary

In short, capitalism is expanding and causing major changes in the structure, cohesion and functioning of the world economy. These changes are leading to a more intense interweaving of economies, with increased interdependence as the result. National economies are more closely linked to one another, which leads, among other things, to a greater synchronisation or coordination of economic ebbs and flows. The world's production and consumption patterns are becoming more mutually interdependent. In general, markets for goods, services, capital and financial instruments and, to a lesser extent, labour are more integrated worldwide.

At the microlevel as well – the level of a single firm – internationalisation is increasing. As a result companies are less dependent on one country or a few countries when they decide on the location of their markets, personnel and operating units; multinationals place different parts of their production in widely separated countries; and they move parts, raw materials, semi-finished goods and finished products incessantly around the world.

National states have less of a grip on economic developments, and governments and parliaments are consciously renouncing control over the movement of goods, services and capital across frontiers. The weakening of the national states' grip on the economy is not being compensated by stronger international regulatory bodies or by a global central bank. Consequently, the likelihood of crises that spread like oil spills due to the international interconnection of economies and companies is growing – as witnessed with the outbreak and spread of crises in Southeast Asia after mid-1997.

Contrary to the reigning economic dogmas, according to which as much as possible should be left to the market, the 'invisible hand' that is supposed to bring the market smoothly back into balance has to be regularly lent a helping hand by governments, central bankers and international organisations like the BIS and the IMF. The BIS, for example, came up with a binding regulation in 1988 – after prolonged negotiations – which internationally operating banks must keep to in determining the composition of their capital reserves. The BIS also adopted a directive on how banks should calculate the reserves they need in order to cover possible losses on the financial markets, including derivatives. The IMF has lent the crisis-plagued states of Southeast Asia, Russia and Brazil tens of billions of dollars – which they will have to pay back – in order to prevent the snowballing of all the different financial crises into a worldwide crisis of the financial system.

Compared to the increased financial instability, however, these are very modest and above all reactive steps.

To the extent that central banks and governments intervene at all with regulations, they limit themselves to those measures that are most essential to avoid the worst disasters. As a matter of principle they leave the markets themselves as free as possible, with all the effects and risks this entails. All the discussions in the wake of the Asian crisis about the 'international financial architecture' have not changed this pattern at all. Established interests and mainstream policymakers and their advisers only want to make liberalised financial makers safer for investors and speculators. They certainly do not want to see any alteration in the world economy's hegemonic logic and machinery.

The Down Side

Environmental groups and radical left organisations in the EU who opposed the Maastricht Treaty for social or ecological reasons, or those in non-member states who have campaigned against joining the EU, have discovered that many people's first associations with increased European integration are positive. Almost everyone is in principle for more international cooperation, fewer hassles during trips and an expanded field of cultural vision. Ideas like a common currency and eliminating restrictions on movement across boundaries elicit considerable sympathy.

The same is true of globalization. In principle it sounds good, in times when no single major social problem – pollution or migration or unemployment – can conceivably be solved inside the boundaries of a single country. There also seem to be many advantages to it. 'Even more than technological progress, globalisation is almost always presented as a necessary and beneficial process.'[43] Products are supposedly becoming cheaper and can be obtained more quickly and in greater variety. According to the economic and political mainstream, everyone will gain in the end from free trade, free movement of capital and internationalised markets and companies.

But when examined more closely, many hymns of praise to globalization are mainly ideology. In reality, globalization has far-reaching negative effects.[44]

To begin with, there is a striking contrast between the pretty stories – about more intensive cooperation, win-win situations and improved living standards for everyone as a result of globalization – and the frankly warlike rhetoric of governments, companies and in some cases union leaders in defence of their particular national or corporate interests. There are countless examples: Clinton threatens the Japanese with sanctions unless Japan admits more US cars; Boeing wages battle with a European consortium in order to get its foot in the door of China's market for a new generation of aircraft; the Dutch government presents its tax system overhaul as extremely competitive with the rest of the EU; the US calls on the WTO to make the EU admit more Del Monte bananas; the EU threatens Japan with a WTO procedure unless Japan changes the tariff structures in its ports; since the end of the Cold War the CIA is devoting a great part of its budget to economic espionage.[45]

One round of negotiations and conferences follows another in order to exorcise (threats of) trade wars, protectionism, quotas, industrial espionage, violation of patent rights, product norms in restraint of free trade and free-trade agreements among a few countries that hinder global free trade. Behind the idyllic facade of an economically unifying world lurk major conflicts of interests and battles over markets, raw materials, jobs and profits. Multinationals try to safeguard their competitive positions by defending their existing market shares, pushing down costs and winning new markets. They are backed in their stratagems by their host countries' governments, which, among other things, fight on 'their own' multinationals' behalf in international organisations and forums for the most favourable treaties and rules possible.

However much economists demonstrate conclusively with graphs, differential comparisons and computer models that globalization and increased free trade lead to win-win situations, their exercises often have little to do with reality.[46] Calculations showing NAFTA's benefits for US, Canadian and Mexican workers, for example, were based on totally

unrealistic hypotheses: full employment and capital immobility.[47]

Reality is usually quite different. Higher profits through
lowered costs come at the expense of wages and jobs. A larger
market share for one company means a shrinking or stagnant
market share for others. Opening up a previously protected
market to foreign companies through the pressure of international treaties and economic blackmail leads to loss of
employment, of economic and social networks and of traditional know-how.

In contrast to repeated claims in glossy reports and investigations, this is also true of the 1994 GATT agreement. A
frequently cited OECD study estimated that the treaty would
lead to a worldwide increase in trade of $200 to $300 billion.
But the bitter truth is that little of this money is finding its way
to the Third World. Furthermore, OECD Secretary-General
Jean-Claude Paye himself called the study 'very theoretical'.
The media devoted too little attention to the conclusion that
the predicted benefits would come only after ten years, said
Paye, and that some developing countries would even be
harmed by the GATT treaty.[48] An UNCTAD study came to
the conclusion that, as a result of the Uruguay Round, the
world's 48 poorest countries would lose $300 to $600 million
a year in decreased exports and increased food imports.[49]

Dictatorship of the financial markets

International capital movements are increasing at an unprecedented rate, but that does not mean that it is any easier to
attract capital. The reverse is true: thanks to the internationalisation of capital markets and the liberalisation of capital
flows, the suppliers of capital, always in search of higher
returns, are making and breaking many governments:

> More telling for our future than ignorant armies that clash
> by night are savvy 24-hour financial traders who, with the
> tap of a keyboard, can attack a weak currency or sound the
> retreat of global capital from a nation's ill-considered tax
> hike. We live, after all, in an age when the White House

fears not hostile communists but bellicose bond traders, and when statesmen like South African President Nelson Mandela talk not of settling old scores but ... of seeking new investment.[50]

It has been a long time since only economically weak countries suffered under the financial markets' dictatorship. When New Zealand's ruling National Party was threatened with the loss of its parliamentary majority in the 1994 by-elections, the financial markets reacted immediately with falling exchange rates, rising interest rates and falling share prices. Prime Minister Bolger warned of 'economic chaos'. Calm only returned to the markets when the opposition Alliance Party hastily announced that the National Party should continue to govern even if it lost its majority.[51] Even the supposedly mighty euro had to contend with falling exchange rates in June 1999, less than half a year after its introduction, because traders disapproved of a slight increase in the Italian budget deficit from 2.0 to 2.4 per cent.

The conclusion is that those who want to attract capital or investors on the global financial market have to adapt to the demands and wishes of the suppliers of capital; otherwise the party is off. Countries in every part of the world, above all in the Third World, Eastern Europe and the former Soviet Union, are thus pressurised to adapt their macroeconomic, fiscal and monetary policies to the 'market's' demands. Indeed, when it comes to evaluating economic developments and profit prospects in non-OECD countries, traders and speculators give considerable weight to the IMF and World Bank's recommendations, demands and marks awarded. The IMF has one prescription for all Third World and Eastern European countries: it advises (or forces) them to prioritise export expansion and payment of foreign debt. The result for these countries is a very lopsided economic structure. Their domestic populations' interests and needs remain neglected as long as their governments do not see or do not opt for a way out of the IMF's straitjacket.

Around the world tens of thousands of well-paid researchers, consultants and experts devote all their time every day to interpreting reports, statistics, balance sheets,

year-end figures and news releases and to calculating
investors' and speculators' chances. This is a wholly unpro-
ductive waste of large quantities of knowledge, energy and
money. The social effects of the immense monetary flows
splashing furiously back and forth around the world play no
role in these cold calculations. 'We went into Latin America
not knowing anything about the place,' said a fund manager
after the outbreak of the Mexican peso crisis in December
1994. 'Now we are leaving without knowing anything about
it.'[52] According to the reigning economic orthodoxy, liberalised financial markets lead to an 'optimal allocation of financial resources'; but 'optimal' means 'most profitable'. The
'invisible hand' of the financial markets strangles billions of
people and entire countries.

> It takes too much blind faith in markets to believe that the
> global allocation of resources is enhanced by the twenty-
> something-year-olds in London who move hundreds of
> millions of dollars around the globe in a matter of an
> instant, or by the executives of multinational enterprises
> who make plant-location decisions on the basis of the
> concessions they can extract from governments.[52]

Race to the bottom

As markets become more and more integrated and international, and restrictions and controls on the cross-boundary
flow of goods, services and capital are rapidly eliminated,
wages, working conditions, employment and social security
risk being sucked into a downwards spiral. The English firm
Morgan Crucible, for instance, decided to produce less in the
Netherlands, Belgium and France and more in the Czech
Republic, Vietnam and China in order to push its 1997 rate
of return above 14 per cent. The Morgan Crucible director,
Farmer, calculated that the company only had to pay
employees in Shanghai $1 a day, as opposed to $31 a day in
Japan.[54] By shifting production to countries with lower wages
and with fiscally more attractive policies, or by importing
cheap goods from low-wage countries – or simply by threat-

ening to do so – employers can keep working conditions under permanent pressure, and companies making billions in profits can shrink their work force year in and year out.[55] Freer trade in goods, services, technology and capital without any international norms leaves the door open for development based on low wages. 'Yet despite the cheaper labor, the primacy of the money markets denies us full employment.'[56]

The official Dutch Social-Economic Council has warned of a process of 'levelling down' on a European scale:

> Neither a 'race to the bottom' with government policies that are non-productive (in the short term) nor a 'race to the top' with 'productive' government policies can be considered beneficial in the long term. The 'dismantling' of social security systems or health care, for example, can have not only negative social consequences but also negative economic consequences over time ... In the field of fiscal policy, lack of adequate coordination could also lead to each government's trying to lure capital and industry – more generally, mobile factors of production – to its own country by means of an attractive fiscal climate.[57]

The ongoing global race for more markets and higher profits is leading to continual cost-cutting: shrinkage of work forces and savings on wage costs and social security expenditure. This is new: 'The old saw has changed: Now, in good times companies will fire. In bad times they'll fire even more.'[58] Also new is the fact that not only unskilled jobs are eliminated, but also middle-level management, skilled and better-paying jobs. Job elimination has reached such proportions that *The Economist* and *Business Week* speak of the 'anorexic company': companies obsessed with cost-cutting, with the motto, 'No pain, no gain.' No end to this trend is in sight. Many companies are constantly in the midst of restructuring. There is a fashion for 'greenfielding' or 're-engineering', which means: think how you would set up a company if you were starting from scratch today, and adapt your existing company's organisation and functioning to fit the model.

According to some estimates 25 million jobs must disappear in the United States out of a private-sector total of 90 million ... Baden-Württemburg's ex-premier Heinrich Henzler ... has announced that 9 million out of Germany's 33 million jobs can disappear without decreasing production if the best technical achievements are applied wherever possible.[59]

These are fundamental changes with far-reaching effects. The phenomenon of 'delocalisation of production' has broken the links between high technology, high labour productivity, high quality and high wages.[60] This coupling seemed in the past to guarantee rising living standards in industrialised countries; but today high technology, high labour productivity and high quality can be combined with low wages. The consequences of the resulting murderous competition are visible to everyone. Economists and politicians nonetheless continue to reassure us that, if we bite the bullet now and patiently hold the course, everything will get better in the long run. Unfortunately, as Keynes noted years ago: 'In the long run we are all dead.'

Privatisation

Companies all over the world are being privatised on a grand scale, not only in OECD countries, but also in the Third World. Between 1988 and 1992, for example, 25 developing countries privatised a total of $61.6 billion worth of companies. The state's role is being redefined. The World Bank is encouraging Third World governments to privatise still more, in order to make their economies more efficient. However,

No scholar in the world has ever succeeded in demonstrating that service provision by the private sector is less expensive overall than by the public sector. Privatisation is above all an expression of the *Zeitgeist* and the rise of the new right ... There is no general scientific rationale for it.[61]

Urged on by employers and the European employers' organisation UNICE, European Union member states are also privatising one company after another. There is a world-wide trend to which at the moment no end is in sight. But the disadvantages are gradually beginning to become clear. There was a virtual general strike in Belgium in November 1994 to protest against job losses resulting from anticipated privatisation. Dutch MP Adrie Duivesteijn has pointed out the disastrous consequences of the state's withdrawal from the housing market:

> The Netherlands was once the least expensive country to rent in in Europe. With the coming round of rent increases we will become the most expensive country to rent in ... Low-income people are being housed in a steadily shrinking part of the housing stock. Housing has become the driving force behind physical segregation in Dutch cities.[62]

A commission chaired by the former Dutch Labour Party president, Sint, harshly criticised privatisations carried out in the Netherlands:

> The state was supposed to become smaller. And of course better. But while politicians were formulating noble goals to justify privatising services, the bureaucracy was fumblingly putting another state together: no smaller than before, but definitely more expensive, and for the most part exempted from any political control. Nobody supervised the process; no one kept track of its effects.[63]

One reason for the wave of privatisations is the fact that governments can earn money by selling off public companies. That was important in the EU in order to reduce national budget deficits to the levels required by the Maastricht Treaty and the Stability Pact. Governments also save the money that might have been needed to continue subsidising services. This makes tax cuts possible, and the countries in question attractive to investors. The negative effects of this dynamic can also be substantial. Privatised companies must make profits in order to satisfy investors, and in the end this makes products less affordable, service provision worse and employment levels lower. The privatised British railways are a notorious example. Another example is the Dutch telephone company, which within half a year of its triumphant entry into the stock market announced the elimination of 3000 jobs so as to remain competitive with the rest of the world.

Increasing migration

Migratory flows and numbers of refugees are increasing around the world. The liberalisation and internationalisation of goods and capital movements are an important cause of this, even though Western governments in particular are doing everything they can to slow migration. Their policies were very different in the years between 1870 and 1914, a time with which today's period of globalization is often compared. In those years not only capital and goods movements were substantial, but the movement of people across boundaries also grew very considerably.[64] Today, contrary to what many people think, the great majority of refugees flee within their own parts of the world. In Western Europe, where per capita GNP varies between $15,000 and $30,000 a year, asylum seekers comprise 0.3 per cent of the population; in Malawi, with a per capita income of $180, they make up 10 per cent of the population.

By official count there were 17 million refugees and asylum seekers in the world in 1992. Of that number, 13.2 million (78 per cent) were in the Third World, and about 2 million refugees from former Yugoslavia remained in European countries located nearby (Croatia, Serbia, Slovenia, Hungary, Austria and Germany). In addition, roughly 4 million people in the Third World were living in refugee-type conditions, and the total number of 'internally displaced' people – those who had fled their homes for safer places inside their own countries – was estimated at 23 million. Fewer than 5 per cent of the world's 'involuntary displaced' people were in Western Europe or North America.[65]

The current increase in numbers of migrants and refugees must be seen as the outcome of various historical processes which have their own rhythm and dynamic. The process of globalization has stimulated the increase in migration and refugees in various ways. To begin with, new connections, structures and networks have arisen through the internationalisation of economies. It is logical that the growth of international movement of capital, goods and people is accompanied by a growth in the movement of people across boundaries. It is hypocritical of the great majority of neoliberal politicians and economists to shrink from the consequences of the pro-market reforms that they have been preaching.

The internationalisation of production has led to new or altered relationships between industrialised and Third World countries.[66] As a result, people are uprooted, are impelled to migrate or come to see migration to a country to which they are linked economically as desirable and feasible. Major cities also function as coordination and management centres for the world economic system; there is a demand there for low-paid, often insecure work which is often consigned to migrants.

A second factor is that stable social relationships in much of the Third World and Eastern Europe have collapsed due to globalization. In many countries of the Third World and the former Soviet Union, civil society was underdeveloped. The state bore the responsibility for social cohesion and political stability, and the weakening of the state has led to a major sharpening of social, religious and ethnic tensions. Conflicts resulting in part from these changes have produced and are producing large numbers of refugees and displaced people.[67]

Finally, globalization has also meant changes in the industrialised OECD countries themselves. The introduction of new technologies, the process of dismantling the gains of the welfare state, the growing flexibility and job insecurity for large parts of the work force, and growing social differentiation have led to a new segmentation of the labour market along lines of gender, ethnicity, nationality and citizenship. Roughly 500 illegal garment sweatshops were counted in Amsterdam in 1993, for example. Employers are glad to hire undocumented immigrants in various other sectors as well, since they are cheap, unprotected and easy to get rid of. Changes in the structure and functioning of the industrialised countries' economies thus leads to increased migration. There is a growing demand for cheap labour in contemporary

European economies, and the demand can be met in part with unregulated labour. Undocumented workers – 'migrant labour' as well as asylum seekers who have been turned down or gone underground – are an important source.

Policies aimed at preventing (illegal) immigration may very well lead to further development of a 'black market' in labour. It is no surprise in any case that a pro-immigration lobby exists in the US and Europe. Spokespeople for agricultural, construction, hotel and restaurant and ready-to-wear industries have made pro-immigration statements. The European Round-table, a major lobby of European transnational enterprises, has also suggested that there would be advantages to expanding the possibilities for (temporary) labour migration.[68]

Growing social inequality

The effects of two decades of neoliberal globalization are clearest in the field of social differences. Increasing income inequality is a worldwide trend. In England the differences in income between upper and lower social layers are larger than they have ever been since collection of income distribution statistics began at the end of the nineteenth century. In the US, income inequality has grown considerably since the 1980s: between 1977 and 1989, 60 per cent of income growth benefited the richest 1 per cent of the population.[69] Between 1989 and 1995 in the US the real incomes of the 80 per cent of men with the lowest earnings and the 70 per cent of women with the lowest earnings either stagnated or declined.[70] In New Zealand, where various governments have carried out very austere social policies since the early 1980s, the number of people eating the Salvation Army's free meals rose 1114 per cent between 1991 and 1994. It is no wonder that malnutrition and diseases like scurvy are once more to be found in New Zealand.[71]

Before the outbreak of the Asian crisis in 1997, UNCTAD Secretary-General Rubens Ricupero noted that, while the economies of the developing countries as a whole had been growing faster in the 1990s than the relatively slow-growing OECD economies, this was mainly due to the then high growth rates in East Asia. In Latin America growth was less sustained and lower, while in Africa per capita income continued to fall in the 1990s as it had in the 1980s. This hardly rosy picture became still more disheartening when income and wealth distribution was examined:

> The big story of the world economy since the early 1980s has been the unleashing of market forces ... The 'invisible hand' now operates globally and with fewer countervailing pressures from governments than for decades. Many commentators are optimistic about the prospects for faster growth and for convergence of incomes and living standards which greater global competition should bring. However, there is also another big story. Since the early 1980s the world economy has been characterized by rising inequality and slow growth.[72]

This assertion is easily buttressed with facts. In 1960 the average income of the richest 20 per cent of the world's population was 30 times higher than that of the poorest 20 per cent; but in 1995 this disproportion had grown to 82:1.[73] Ricupero calculated in his 1997 report that average income in Africa had fallen steadily during the previous three decades, to barely 7 per cent of the industrialised countries' average. Average income in Latin America fell from over a third of that of the industrialised North at the end of the 1970s to a quarter of the industrialised North's level. Only a handful of East Asian countries seemed at the time to have succeeded in narrowing the gap or even joined the North; but since the outbreak of the Asian crisis in 1997 it is these very prodigies that have been demoted to total losses.

Polarisation between countries is accompanied moreover by increasing inequality within countries. In more than half the developing countries the richest 20 per cent of the population now receives more than 50 per cent of the national income. In many countries the incomes of the poorest 20 per cent are now less than 10 per cent of the incomes of the richest 20 per cent.

These trends are not accidental; they are the result of the forces let loose by the far-reaching liberalisation of the world economy. Various factors are working in favour of high-income groups and leading to greater inequality: income differences have increased in almost all developed countries as well; capital has gained at the expense of labour, given that the share of profits in national incomes has risen sharply; a new class of rentiers has arisen as a result of financial liberalisation and profits from the immense growth of international capital flows and from high real interest rates. Those who claim, expect or honestly hope that the negative effects of globalization are only temporary phenomena that will disappear in the long run are firmly disabused by the UNCTAD Secretary-General's report:

> [E]vidence is mounting that slow growth and rising inequalities are becoming more permanent features ... It is this association of increased profits with stagnant investment, rising unemployment and reduced pay that is the real cause for concern ... Corporate restructuring, labour shedding and wage repression in this world of sluggish growth have thus become the order of the day, generating increased job and income insecurity.[74]

In short, increasing liberalisation, deregulation, privatisation, flexibility and internationalisation – all the characteristics of the process of economic globalization under way since the late 1970s – clearly do not lead to a convergence of different countries' widely different levels of development. On the contrary, they are leading to increasing social differences both within and among countries. Advocates of today's neoliberal internationalisation cannot make the claim that it leads to economic convergence.[75]

We must nonetheless remember that neoliberal globalization has brought not only great suffering, but also great riches, above all to people in upper income brackets, corporations and the new rentiers. Its most extreme and perverse result is the unprecedented concentration of wealth in fewer and fewer hands. The combined wealth of the world's 225 richest people, over $1 trillion, equals the combined annual incomes of the world's poorest 2.5 billion inhabitants. Four per cent of this amount – roughly $40 billion a year – is the estimated 'additional cost of achieving and maintaining universal access to basic education for all, basic health care for all, reproductive health care for all women, adequate food for all and safe water and sanitation for all'.[76]

It is easy to see how globalization has led to this growing social inequality. While incomes, working conditions and social security are under downwards pressure from global competition, capital owners' ability to seek out the most profitable investments almost anywhere in the world is increasing. While privatisation leads to declining service provision and employment, the privatised companies provide attractive investment opportunities for capital owners. In this way the rise of an ethnically segmented social hierarchy is built into the logic of globalization.

This is also apparent from the speed with which the former Eastern bloc is being 'integrated'. Income inequality in Hungary, for example – not one of the poorer Eastern European countries – has increased sharply since 1992. The best-paid 10 per cent now receives 25 per cent of gross income, while the poorest 10 per cent gets only 3.8 per cent. Rising unemployment and income inequality and declining real wages, pension and unemployment benefits have led to a growing number of people living at or below subsistence level.[77] Comparisons among Eastern European countries show that GNP has fallen further and faster where IMF programmes were implemented.[78] Yet the IMF continues to defend harsh interventions in Eastern Europe and the former Soviet Union with the fewest possible social measures to soften the blow, on the grounds that maintaining 'or attempting to maintain a comprehensive welfare state ... could very well delay or make impossible a shift to a dynamic growing economy'.[79]

Globalization is male

There is another cumulative effect of the factors mentioned above to which little or no attention is paid: The position of many women in particular is getting worse.[80] Women's organisations have concluded from this fact that the global economy is a man. For example, 67.2 per cent of the world's work is done by women, while only 9.4 per cent of the income earned from work is in women's hands. Despite great regional differences, it is possible to identify a number of globalization's general effects on women:[81]

Increased economic integration has led to a worldwide contradictory process of proletarianisation of women. Women are driven into the army of labour, but at the same time their role in the family and society is used to justify insecure jobs, irregular working hours and the return of many personal services to the family where women are responsible for them.

Work: Many women work in free-trade zones that have been set up all over the world by and for multinationals, for example, in the Mexican *maquiladoras* and the so-called informal sector. This *'maquiladorisation'* of women's work in both Third World and developed countries undermines their right to decent working conditions, pensions, pregnancy leave and positive action programmes.

Health and welfare: Changes in working conditions and decreased safety at work directly affect women's health and welfare and 'the welfare of those family members (especially children and the elderly) for whom women are primarily responsible'. In addition, rising prices and increasing unemployment make it harder for women to meet their basic needs, while state support for education, health care and child care is being decreased through cutbacks on social and collective programmes. These developments are particularly bad for women 'because of their central role in both biological and social reproduction'. The state also 'depends on women to "take up the slack" and provide on a private basis services that were previously provided by the government'.

Social gains and basic rights: Economic restructuring has negative effects on the social gains women made in the past 25 years, such as abortion rights, the right to equal pay and the right to freedom from sexual harassment and violence.

Sexuality: In addition to attacks on women's rights to control their own reproduction, trade in women, sex tourism and the international sex trade are on the rise.

Ideology: Among the ideological changes resulting from globalization that have an impact on women are the effects of the great emphasis on individualism and privatisation, and 'the possibility that NAFTA and the EU will play a role in undermining both memories of and aspirations for progressive national struggles. This in turn could have special implications for women, since it is through such struggles that women's demands are frequently raised and secured.'

Women and their organisations are increasingly launching international initiatives against these gender-specific effects of globalization, such as the Women's Global March planned for 2000.

Ecological effects

Increased internationalisation of production also has serious ecological effects. Multinationals are shipping products and parts to the ends of the earth and back in order to supply them as cheaply as possible. By definition, under capitalism social and ecological costs for present and future generations play no role in decisions about investments, location of production and what is produced. Individual employers also make these decisions without reference to one another. Their only criterion is what is rational and profitable from the standpoint of their own narrow interests. Lower transport costs and new technologies and institutional and political changes have made transnational and transcontinental trade and production easier, cheaper and more realistic for them. As a result, internationalisation of goods and services production has reached an unprecedented scale. This logic is changing the structure of many industries. It can lead to truly absurd situations:

> A few years ago, I was eating at a restaurant in Saint Paul, Minnesota. After lunch I picked up a toothpick wrapped in plastic. On the plastic was the word 'Japan'. Now Japan has little wood and no oil. Yet in our global economy, it is deemed efficient to send little pieces of wood and some barrels of oil to Japan, wrap the one in the other and send them back to Minnesota. This toothpick may embody 50,000 miles of travel. Meanwhile, in 1987, a Minnesota

factory began producing millions of disposable chopsticks a year for sale in Japan. In my mind's eye, I see two ships passing on another in the northern Pacific. One carries little pieces of Minnesota wood bound for Japan; the other carries little pieces of wood from Japan bound for Minnesota. Such is the logic of free trade.[82]

But there is more. Capital's increased mobility makes it harder and harder for citizens to organise themselves and use their governments to restrain polluting companies and impose rules. Environmental organisations rightly object to the single global market and the WTO. Trade liberalisation encourages a particular type of economic growth – the current, wasteful type – and leads in this way to still more environmental destruction.

It has become more difficult for countries to institute stricter environmental requirements for products. The safety requirements for food are higher in the US than international norms, but as a result of the WTO treaty Brazil, for example, can ship fruit sprayed with DDT and other chemicals to the US even if the pesticides are not permitted by US law. Brazil can simply argue before the WTO in Geneva that the US requirements restrain trade. If applied completely consistently, this would lead to a complete elimination of product norms.[83] The WTO treaty no longer allows countries to keep out products because of how they were produced or harvested. The treaty also prevents countries from restricting exports of goods, animals or products that they want to protect, such as tropical wood or elephants. The WTO can sabotage international environmental agreements by banning measures which restrain trade. Global free trade will also lead to a levelling of environmental norms for products down to the lowest level, since everything must be produced as cheaply as possible in order to stay competitive.

Elimination of trade restraints and restrictions thus leads to greater worldwide freedom to pollute – all the more since there is now an integrated world market for toxic waste disposal. International trade in dangerous wastes is increasing, with more and more junk being dumped in poor countries. Between 1989 and 1994 there were over 500 attempts to dump more than 200 million tonnes of rubbish from the 24 rich OECD countries in 122 non-OECD countries. For example, the government of Guinea-Bissau agreed in 1988 to allow the dumping of 15 million tonnes of toxic waste in its territory in return for $600 million, four times the country's gross national product. Asked for an explanation, the minister of trade and tourism said: 'We need the money.'[84]

Undermining democracy

Another result of the current economic globalization is the undermining of democracy. The NAFTA treaty can serve as an illustration of a more general process: in the treaty, 'the market' is solemnly confirmed as the principle according to which economic activity in North America must be organised. This is implemented through the establishment of basic rules, bans on government action to advance the public sector and restrictions on governmental power to regulate the private sector effectively (by limiting or ruling out certain types of regulation and by giving companies more loopholes through which rules can be evaded). In this way NAFTA restricts democracy by restricting people's ability to exercise political control over their own economic lives.[85]

The same holds true for the EU: its European Central Bank is independent and unaccountable, so European monetary policy is now beyond the reach of any democratic control or influence. The same story can be told about the WTO; the organisation has all sorts of powers and abilities to take action against disobedient countries and governments. Ralph Nader has come out in particular against the WTO; one country can lodge a complaint about another country's laws before a WTO tribunal in Geneva, and if the complainant wins – the defendant country must prove its innocence – then the defendant country must change its laws, pay fines or accept sanctions being taken against it.[86]

Financial markets and unaccountable international institutions are acquiring more and more power and influence. The trend towards independence and autonomy for national and international organisations has been called the 'new constitutional discourse':

The discourse concerns institutional arrangements designed to insulate key economic agencies, especially central banks, from the interference of elected politicians, who, it is argued, have a tendency in liberal democracies to inflate the economy for electoral purposes or to use the 'inflation tax' to indirectly improve the government's financial position. For example, the former UK Chancellor of the Exchequer, Nigel Lawson, who engineered an inflationary boom to win the 1987 General Election for the Conservatives in Britain, is now in favour of independent banks and a strengthening of the GATT and IMF surveillance.[87]

More generally, transfers of power and authority to bureaucratic international organisations and trading blocs that take their decisions behind closed doors mean that our future is being determined behind our backs or beyond our reach by 'the market' or unaccountable 'authorities'. The EU's 'democratic deficit', not to speak of the IMF's or the BIS's, is chronic; it cannot be eliminated within the existing constellation of forces.

'Commodification'

In conclusion, one other way must be mentioned in which globalization has a major impact on people's daily lives. The steadily greater reach of the market is reinforcing the process of 'commodification', through which everything is reduced to a product to be bought and sold. 'Market relations are insistently praised as the most desirable form of individual and social interaction; and there has never been a time when commercialization has more thoroughly come to pervade all spheres of life.'[88]

Human relationships are becoming more and more businesslike. For many people 'solidarity' has become an old-fashioned, discredited concept – and no wonder, when it is used for arguments such as: 'You should agree to cuts in your wages out of solidarity with the unemployed.' Social links and networks through which people help each other are disintegrating because of poverty, unemployment and the way people and causes are constantly played against each other.

Omnipresent commercialisation means that money can be made by turning more and more things into commodities: patents on animals, plants and human genes;[89] leisure time (television, shopping expeditions, amusement parks for day-trippers, casinos); culture (media commercialisation, corporate sponsorship of museums, exhibits and cultural events); sex (sex tourism, pornography, sex lines) and human organs.[90] Changes in the role of the state play an important part in this commodification. Because the state is financing and organising fewer and fewer social and public services, many aspects of social life like education, health care and culture are being (re-)commodified. Money plays a steadily more important role in people's everyday experience.

The down side: summary

Neoliberal globalization is not the cause of all the world's ills, of course. But global economic developments since the early 1980s undeniably have far-reaching negative consequences for the great majority of the current world population as well as future generations: less access to capital for those who do not meet 'market' criteria; greater social differences as a result of the dual polarisation within countries and on a world scale among countries; growing migration; 'levelling down' of wages, working conditions and social security; ecological damage; further restrictions on democracy; and increasing commodification. This is the down side of the univeral rise in market-based thinking and of the logic of globalization.

Reality, Ideology and Myth

The process of globalization means a qualitatively new phase in the internationalisation of capitalism. But the extent and effects of the changes are often exaggerated, in many cases for political reasons. Many myths are being propagated. It is important therefore not to lose sight of the limits to globalization.

Globalization or triadisation?

The tendency towards globalization is not a linear process and is not leading to a truly homogeneous unification of the world's economies. In reality we are witnessing a vertical restructuring of the world economy around three poles, the so-called Triad – the EU, Japan and the US – which marginalises most of the world: the countries kept in underdevelopment in the Third World, Eastern Europe and the former Soviet Union. This can be seen from the following facts:[91]

- Capital is flowing above all from and to the EU, Japan and the US. In the 1980s the Triad accounted for more than 80 per cent of all capital movements. The share of developing countries fell in the same period from 25 per cent to 19 per cent; in 1976 it was still 30 per cent. In the early 1990s capital flows towards developing countries increased again, and in 1994 total capital flows from industrialised to developing countries (private loans and investments and money from official sources) amounted to $227.4 billion, 6.7 per cent more than in 1993.[92] But most of the money went to a limited core group of ten Asian and Latin American countries.

  Even for countries that are popular with foreign investors, the arrival of capital is far from always positive. Even before the crisis broke out in Mexico at the end of 1994 it was clear that the great majority of arriving capital was speculative capital attracted by privatisations, which did not serve to create anything new. There are also changes under way in capital flows towards developing countries. Investors' preferences and priorities can change quickly. It is thus far from certain that countries that attract capital today can continue to do so tomorrow.
- The great majority of the world's direct investment comes from and ends up in industrialised countries, as shown in Table 1.4.
- Most of the expansion of international trade (about 80 per cent) concerns the developed countries.
- More than 90 per cent of multinational headquarters are in the Triad. Out of the 100 biggest multinationals, 38 have

Table 1.4 Regional distribution of inward and outward FDI stock (%)[93]

| | Inward FDI stock | | |
	Developed countries	Developing countries	Central & Eastern Europe
1985	72.3	27.7	—
1990	79.3	20.6	0.1
1995	70.6	28.1	1.3
1997	68.0	30.2	1.8
	Outward FDI stock		
	Developed countries	Developing countries	Central & Eastern Europe
1985	95.7	4.3	—
1990	95.6	4.4	—
1995	91.5	8.4	0.1
1997	90.2	9.7	0.2

their headquarters in the EU, 29 in the US and 16 in Japan. Most subsidiaries of multinationals are in other developed countries.

• Between 85 and 90 per cent of high-tech products with a high added value are produced and consumed in the Triad, while the New Industrialising Countries (NICs) account for most of the rest.

• Of the registered patents, 85 per cent in the 1980s were registered in five countries: the US, Japan, Germany, Britain and France. Multinationals still do most of their research and development in their mother countries.

In light of these facts globalization should really be called 'triadisation' – even though only 15 per cent of the world's population live in the Triad. As we have seen, no country can escape any more from the pressure and influence of the multi-nationals and international financial markets, but major parts of the world have little or no share in the supposed benefits of global restructuring. Much of the Third World is becoming more and more marginal. In the years 1980–91, per capita GNP grew by an average of 2.3 per cent a year in the OECD countries; for sub-Saharan Africa the figure was -1.2 per cent and for North Africa and the Middle East -2.4 per cent.

Nor is the situation of the great majority in the Third World getting any better. Only a few NICs have been able to develop rapidly, but in many respects these remained dependent, and it is impossible in any event for other countries to follow the same development path.[94] These very same success stories ended in a deep crisis in Asia in mid-1997, moreover, which set these countries far back in their economic development.

The relations of dependency that bind the periphery to the centre continue to exist. They are maintained by various specific mechanisms, including the discipline of the financial markets, but several other mechanisms play a part as well.[95] First, Third World countries are weighed down by a foreign debt that they will never manage to pay off unless much of it is written off. According to the UN, the developing countries' foreign debt grew from $567 billion in 1980 to $1419 billion in 1992. The total debt thus multiplied two and a half times in 12 years – during the same years that the developing countries were paying $771.3 billion in interest and $890.9 in principal, a total of $1662.2 billion, which is three times the original debt in 1980. The trend continued in the 1990s, as total debt grew to $1940 billion in 1995.[96] While the money originally lent has already been paid back twice over and more, the developing countries are saddled with a higher and higher debt. In addition, poor countries have to contend with constantly worsening terms of trade. The total 'invisible transfer' from South to North has been estimated at $200 billion a year.[97]

All this constantly widens the gap between centre and periphery, as has been happening throughout the history of capitalism:

> Globalization is not really global. Transnational business activities are concentrated in the industrial world and in scattered enclaves throughout the underdeveloped world. Most people are outside the system and the ranks of the window-shoppers and the jobless are growing faster than the global army of the employed. Yet the processes of globalization are altering the character of nations everywhere and the quality of life within their borders.[98]

Footloose capital?

Even the largest multinationals are genuinely international in only a limited sense:

> Of the largest one hundred core firms in the world, not one is truly 'global', 'footloose' or 'borderless.' There is however a hierarchy in the internationalisation of functional areas of management; around forty firms generate at least half of their sales abroad; with very few exceptions, executive boards and management styles remain solidly national in their outlook; with even fewer exceptions, R&D remains firmly under domestic control; and most companies appear to think of a globalisation of corporate finances as too uncertain.[99]

Multinationals nonetheless try all too often to extort concessions from governments or unions by threatening to move to another, cheaper country, particularly using the argument that wage costs are too high.[100] This kind of delocalisation does indeed occur; but more often the threat is empty. Wage costs are only 5–10 per cent of total production costs in the most competitive industrial sectors today, down from 25 per cent in the 1970s.[101] Moreover wage costs in themselves – generally compared in terms of costs per employee per hour – mean very little without taking into account how much is produced per employee per hour, that is, labour productivity.[102]

The idea that capital has become completely 'footloose' is not borne out by the facts. Whether large or small, companies depend on national or regional markets, infrastructure (for education, knowledge and research, but also physically for transport) and networks, relationships with unions and governments and often sales patterns that have been built up painstakingly over the years. Companies do not give all this up lightly, nor can they rebuild it all easily in a few weeks somewhere else.

Industrial multinationals therefore do not only pay attention to where wages are the lowest and subsidies highest; they develop a strategy based on the situation on the ground where they are operating. Some companies look above all for an export base where they can manufacture at the lowest possible costs; others try to build up 'globally localised' production and sales networks for specific regions. For these companies the size of national markets, opportunities for trade with neighbouring countries and proximity of clients – so that they can quickly respond to shifts in consumer preferences and provide service – are more important than low costs.[103] Generalisations about companies' strategies for internationalisation are insufficient; concrete analyses of companies and the situation on the ground where they operate are necessary.

Less state, more market?

The final kind of myth concerns the role of the state in the process of globalization. Many politicians say that the state's influence on the economy, and particularly politicians' influence on the economy, must be reduced as much as possible to leave room for the market. 'Less state, more market' is the credo not only of free-marketeers, but also of more and more social-democratic advocates of 'market discipline'. But the reality is very different. The state's influence is not being reduced; it is being given different tasks, but by no means necessarily fewer. While globalization has limited the state's power in some respects, the state's role in other fields has become even bigger.[104]

> In most cases of 'deregulation', governments have combined liberalization with *reregulation*, the reformulation of old rules and the creation of new ones. Hence we have wound up with freer markets and *more* rules. In fact, there is often a logical link: liberalization requires reregulation.[105]

There have been many examples from many countries of this shift in the state's tasks. Under the headline 'The Illusion of French Liberalism', *The European* complained in 1994 that the policy of the right-wing French government of the time was 'becoming more interventionist – not less as promised'.[106] In England, where government programmes were sternly weeded out under Margaret Thatcher, the anti-state offensive often led to 'quasi-autonomous non-governmental organisations (Quangos)' continuing to run services that they had previously run as departments of local government.[107] Free-market champion Ronald Reagan's actions did not correspond to his official ideology either. The state did not do less under his administration, but partially changed its priorities:

> However, despite his emphasis on limiting the growth of government, Reagan was not successful in cutting government spending. Instead, the character of government spending changed considerably in the 1980s. In the year before Reagan took office, defense spending accounted for 22.7 percent of total federal outlays. In 1988, when Reagan left office, this figure had risen to 27.3 percent. In contrast, the percentage of federal outlays going to social services and income security both decreased by 2.4 percent over the same period ... This restructuring of federal government spending had significant effects on women both in terms of employment opportunities as well as available services.[108]

The state always carries out a number of crucial economic functions under capitalism – guaranteeing property rights, standardising monetary units and weights and measures, coordinating the economy, helping guarantee inputs into the economic process (work force, subsidies, technological development, infrastructure), maintaining relations with other states, and last but not least organising a social consensus[109] – but does so in varying ways and with varying intensity. It has various instruments at its disposal, and does not have to carry out its tasks on its own. A Swiss multinational that sets up a company in the Netherlands can rely on the Dutch state to carry out the economic functions that are necessary for the company's operations; it does not need any direct intervention by the Swiss state. States can also delegate major tasks to the private sector. They can of course work together in international organisations and transfer their authority to those organisations.

How and by whom state tasks are carried out and what their tasks consist of is not fixed for all eternity. It depends on concrete economic, social, political and institutional developments. The internationalisation of the world economy has led to states working together more in international institutions. But international organisations like the EU cannot function in a vacuum; they need their national member states to establish the legitimacy of their decisions and compel citizens to obey them.

So while governments are cutting back on social and collective programmes and hacking away at the roots of the Western European welfare state – aided by the ideological and organisational weakness of the left – the state's activities are increasing in other fields. States are spending enormous sums of taxpayers' money to save banks in crisis,[110] keep immigrants out and hunt down undocumented workers, suppress workers' resistance when considered necessary (as Thatcher did with the miners and Reagan with the air traffic controllers), invest on a large scale in infrastructural projects (the Channel tunnel, high-speed trains, new and bigger airports) to make their countries more attractive to investors, fund research and development and link higher education to it more closely, lower taxes and raise subsidies in order to make employers happy.

In short, the state's role is being redefined, not reduced. Rhetoric about the disappearing state is largely ideology used to justify cuts in social spending, breaking up the public sector and the one-sided increase in profits that established interests are able to realise through the financial markets.[111]

Scope and Limits

Once again: Is there really anything new under the sun? We have seen how the tendency towards globalization is expressed in various ways and how it means a definite acceleration in the internationalisation of capitalism. The process has major consequences for the functioning of the world economy and national states, and present and future negative effects on much of the world's population. Anyone who reads articles or books about globalization can see that much fashionable, ideological rhetoric is tossed about, all of it to the effect that sooner or later everything will be different and better, now that technological breakthroughs have united the world and forced everyone to respect the 'healthy discipline' of the market. Reality has nothing to do with this rhetoric. It is of utmost importance to analyse economic globalization's real effects, limits and contradictions.

The internationalisation of the world economy is taking place unevenly, because the effects of globalization vary in different countries. It is a contradictory process because globalization runs up against all sorts of counter-tendencies, contradictions and existing interests. Despite the strong trend towards globalization, therefore, no fully integrated world economy has come into existence (yet). All sorts of protectionism are still perceptible; the labour market in particular can hardly be considered a global market. The world is considerably more globalised than 50 years ago, but much less than is theoretically possible. Along with and partly as a result of continuing globalization, the world will still be the scene in coming years of conflicts and contradictions among the rich countries, between different trading blocs, between Third World and OECD countries, and between developing and Eastern European countries on the one hand and the IMF and World Bank on the other.

The outcome of all these developments is open, since supranational institutions that can adequately direct or control today's internationalised world economy are not emerging naturally or automatically. The absence of regulation on an international level creates a great risk of rapidly spreading international crises. In part because governments have themselves given up much of the authority and regulatory tools that they used to have, individual countries now are or seem too big to solve small problems and too small to effectively solve big problems. This can in future lead to uncontrollable situations and further chaos.

CHAPTER 2

Globalization: A Product of Technological Change?

> ... Imagine that we had a government that didn't care
> about technological development ... You could argue
> about how it would have happened and how long it would
> have taken, but it is certain that Dutch society would never
> have survived. We can draw a couple of important conclu-
> sions from this. First, that there is no way to stop the appli-
> cation of new technology ... Second, that government
> policy is largely a prisoner of technological development ...
> Third, that technological development is leading to
> profound cultural change. And the changed culture is in
> turn preparing us to accept still newer technology.
>
> Marcel van Dam[1]

Anyone who goes looking for the causes of the accelerating
internationalisation of economies since the early 1980s must
consider the scope and effects of technological change. In
most explanations of increasing globalization, technology
plays a decisive role. Management gurus, politicians and
economists agree in portraying globalization as an automatic
– and therefore unavoidable – product of technological innovations, notably in the transport sector, telecommunications
and automation.

But is this true? The question is important not only to our
understanding of the world, but also because the answer has
implications for social change and protest. If technological
development is in itself the cause of globalization, then social
protest hardly has any point at all.

Intuitively, it is easy to understand why this kind of technological determinism is not in fact valid. If technology were

the driving force behind globalization, then, how can the fact that there was less international trade for decades after the First World War than there was before 1914 be explained? Even more difficult, how can the fact that the whole period from 1914 to about 1970 was one of 'illiberality in capital markets, with significant restrictions imposed by governments on international capital flows', be understood?[2]

The truth is that technological change has only facilitated globalization processes set in motion by conscious political decisions, pioneered by right-wing US and British governments, from the early 1970s to the early 1980s. These decisions blew up the postwar Bretton Woods system of fixed exchange rates and controlled capital movements, turned much of Europe into a single market and forced the South to open its doors to Northern products and investments. Neoliberalism, far more than technology, made possible the explosion of financial speculation in the last two decades.

Why globalization?

Among the most common explanations for the tendency towards globalization sketched out in the last chapter, a number of elements recur again and again. First, the expansion of markets – both geographical, to countries in the Third World and since 1989 to Eastern Europe, and through commodification – supposedly makes it easier for various industries to produce and sell goods in different countries and continents and to divide activities into pieces that can be spread around the world. The development of a global labour market is important in this regard: the growing number of skilled workers in the world increases the practical possibilities of extending or relocating (parts of) the production and distribution process.

The ability of companies to take advantage of these new opportunities depends on economies of scale that they can benefit from in both production and research and development. In the most advanced sectors greater and greater amounts of money are necessary to develop and market new products or new generations of already existing products, such as microchips. Expanding beyond the boundaries of a single country considerably increases a company's chances of making a profit on a new product line, either independently or jointly with other multinationals. The progressive integration of European countries into the European Union, impelled largely by the needs of capital to make European companies more competitive with Japanese and US rivals, is a good example.

Companies can take advantage of new opportunities because new information and communications technologies and lower transport costs have made it feasible to extend raw materials and semi-finished goods supply networks, as well as production, assembly, distribution and markets, internationally. Owing to various forms of deregulation (of labour markets, requirements for investment, working hours and financial markets) and privatisation, companies in search of attractive investment and sales options can also choose from a broader range of possibilities. These possibilities lead among other things, to an increase in competition among countries in order to attract investors, and a weakening of national governments' hold on 'their own' companies. More and more, the place of 'nations' will be a function of their contribution to multinational actors' competitive advantage', paradoxically as the state increasingly 'affirms its national existence by playing the game of internationalisation'.[3]

The tendency towards globalization is clearly furthest advanced in the financial sector. The international financial revolution has led to 'a dramatic shift in the balance of power away from national and international public authorities towards the private markets'.[4]

Technological changes are important in the financial sector as well: 'Underlying the revolution in global finance is the revolution in communications and information processing which if anything may accelerate over time.'[5] They have made it possible for news of policy changes, reactions to policy changes, economic and financial data, and even news that at first sight has no significance whatsoever for the economy ('sunspots') to lead to immense shifts of funds from one currency or holding to another.

The distinction between banks, other financial institutions and other kinds of companies has also become much hazier. Many companies work with advanced financial management techniques. Many companies, such as Ford, General Motors, Toyota and General Electric, have divisions or subsidiaries that compete with banks. Some multinationals earn more through financial transactions than by producing and selling the products that once made their fortunes.

These various factors have been reinforced by the general decline in economic growth in the industrialised economies since the mid-1970s. Lower potential returns on investment compared with the two previous decades have resulted in less reinvestment of accumulated wealth in the major industrialised countries. Companies now more often have considerable cash reserves at their disposal that they cannot or do not want to invest because they can get a higher rate of return by buying stocks. Increasing quantities of capital are drifting over the face of the earth in search of the highest profits. Institutional investors also have growing amounts of money to play with. This was already happening to a limited extent before the 1970s, but at that point a new stage was reached. The financial sector expanded so quickly from the 1970s on that it was quickly seen as a head swelling out of proportion to the body of the real sector on which it was sitting.

All this could happen only in the wake of the collapse of the Bretton Woods system of fixed exchange rates based on a dollar convertible to gold as an international reserve currency, as a process of far-reaching deregulation of the financial sector and liberalisation of capital flows gathered steam. The volatility of the flexible exchange rates after the collapse of Bretton Woods stimulated the development of financial innovations such as swaps, futures and options. These financial innovations, which weakened national control of cross-border capital movements and financial institutions, as well as growing competition among financial centres, not only heightened instability but also increased the demand for still further liberalisation and deregulation. New frontiers were constantly being sought out, put under pressure and pushed outwards.

Technological Determinism

Various elements play a prominent role in these explanations of growing globalization of production, trade flows and financial markets. Leaving aside a number of pure tautologies, the explanations generally rely on factors that certainly are at work but that are themselves in need of explanation. Why have all these developments been taking place since the early 1980s? Why was globalization not happening, say, 20 years earlier?

In the more comprehensive explanations for the developments that have made globalization possible, one factor is particularly emphasised: technological change is frequently cited as *the* fundamental explanation for globalization. Why this is so is not hard to understand. Wherever we look around us we see a world that appears more and more irrational, chaotic and impenetrable. In the new world order we have steadily less control over our lives and the world around us. Politicians and academics reinforce this impression[6] by writing and saying that society has become so complex that it can no longer be changed by conscious human action.[7] Technological change also plays a very visible role in the shifts we are facing in production and daily life. What could be more obvious than pointing to technology as the cause of globalization and all the other social changes of our time? Isn't technology everywhere, complex, ungraspable and neutral?

The claim that increased globalization is the direct result of technological development is most frequently and plausibly cited as an explanation of the expansion, internationalisation and deregulation of the financial sector. Quantitative and qualitative expansion of electronic media has led to great problems for national regulatory agencies, and the technology and innovations seem to have made everyone and everything take to their heels. If we look at the facts, however, we can see that this claim is untenable, and that financial innovations, application of new technology and deregulation were only made possible by *political* decisions.

Up until the early 1970s, all the major industrialised countries controlled cross-border capital flows. That was a consequence of the agreements reached at Bretton Woods. In reaction to the horrors of the Depression and Second World War, negotiations began during the war over the postwar international economic order. That eventually led in 1944 in Bretton Woods, New Hampshire, to the founding of the IMF and the International Bank for Reconstruction and Development (World Bank). The international trade organisation that was planned at the same time did not come into existence, but international trade negotiating rounds with the goal of lowering trade barriers and tariffs were begun under the auspices of the GATT a few years later.

Bretton Woods was a system of fixed exchange rates. Each country linked its currency in a set ratio to a certain quantity of gold or US dollars; dollars could in turn be traded in for a fixed amount of gold. Exchange rates could be changed, but that was in general unwelcome and before a country was permitted to do so it had to prove that it was contending with 'fundamental disequilibria'.

This system functioned rather well up until the late 1960s. Currency trading was limited to banks that bought and sold foreign currencies at official rates for their clients' foreign trips or international trade. The monetary world was quite comprehensible and simple in those days for central banks as well.

That changed once the Bretton Woods system collapsed. In August 1969 President Nixon suspended the convertibility of the dollar for gold in order to prevent the loss of all US gold reserves. The dollar nonetheless remained the system's most important currency, and when the US formally closed its gold counter for good in August 1971 the world switched in practice to a dollar standard. This situation did not last long, however, because under pressure of increasing capital movements Britain decided in 1972 to let the pound float. Other European countries followed. In the course of 1973 all major currencies were allowed to float.

The switch from fixed to floating exchange rates was followed by a switch from controlled to uncontrolled capital flows. Bretton Woods had been a reaction to the protectionism of the 1930s, primarily aimed at facilitating growth of trade. In order to maintain the system of more or less fixed exchange rates that was considered necessary for trade, and in order to keep domestic economic developments under control, countries maintained controls on cross-border capital movements. These controls were undermined somewhat as early as 1958, when an offshore Eurodollar market arose outside the US; it grew quickly, particularly in the second half of the 1960s.[8] The US government, which wanted to guarantee the dollar's predominance, and the British government, which wanted to profit as much as possible from the City of London's role in the financial world, each contributed in its own interests to the emergence of these offshore markets.[9]

When more and more countries took the step of eliminating capital controls, the whole system fell apart. The US was the first, in January 1974.[10] It was more than five years before Thatcher did the same in Britain. But once she did, Japan, Germany, the Netherlands and other countries rapidly followed suit. Japan did not do so on its own initiative, but began liberalising under US pressure.[11]

The disappearance of postwar capital controls was thus the result of political decisions. These decisions cleared the way for the rapid growth of international financial flows, integration and deregulation of financial markets, and for a stream of derivatives and other financial innovations designed as ways to profit from interest rate variations and exchange rate turbulence, which became much more common after Bretton Woods's collapse. The 1980s were the years of financial revolution. In 1980 futures, swaps and options still barely existed; ten years later there were over seven trillion dollars' worth of these and other financial derivatives in existence around the world.[12]

The liberalisation of capital flows in the EU is also the result of political decisions taken by EU government leaders, consolidated in the European Single Market Act (1985) and Maastricht Treaty (1992), not of the fact that new technologies have made internationalisation of capital flows possible. Participation by a large number of Third World countries in the global race to attract investments and capital has just as little to do with the availability of new technologies as such, and everything to do with targeted pressure from organisations like the World Bank and IMF. These institutions demand implementation of demanding Structural Adjustment Programmes – which impose greater freedom for markets, privatisation, deregulation, wage freezes, lower food subsidies, less spending on health care and education and devaluation of national currencies – by countries that would otherwise be cut off from credits from international organisations and commercial banks.[13]

The frequently told story that financial regulation has become impossible today as a result of technological changes and globalization is also not true. A number of facts make this clear.

First, many of the world's most successful economies have only slowly liberalised their financial markets. That was the case until recently of Japan and South Korea, for example. Countries like India that moved most slowly on financial deregulation were hit far less hard by the 1997 Asian financial crisis, while a hard-hit country like Malaysia has now reimposed partial capital controls without encountering major difficulties.

Second, it still seems well within the realm of possibility to cooperate and regulate where the political will exists, even if liberalisation and internationalisation of financial markets often make it more difficult. Examples are the internationally coordinated attempts to interfere with the laundering of drug money and the international cooperation among central banks when the fraudulent BCCI bank went under in order to survey the damage as quickly as possible. 'There has been no shortage of international cooperation when it has been a matter of freeing markets and limiting the power of democratically elected governments; that priority can be reversed.'[14] This is also evident from the detailed proposals for a so-called 'Tobin tax' on financial transactions.[15]

Third, even the World Bank and IMF sometimes advise Eastern European and Third World countries to liberalise their financial markets more gradually, in order to limit as much as possible the chance of destabilising speculation. These counsels are admissions that limited or gradual deregulation is possible and can be useful.

True, the IMF only considers these exceptional situations in the case of countries which (still) do not have a stable financial system or have to contend with macroeconomic instability. In order to avoid any misunderstanding about which way the wind is blowing, the IMF is revising its statutes. Since 1945 the statutes have said that capital controls are acceptable, but the IMF's top management wants to rewrite that article so as to make unrestricted capital movement a goal for all member countries. The trend is clear. In the mid-1990s between 60 and 70 countries had completely freed capital movements; a decade earlier there were only 20 to 30.[16]

Fourth, everyone has to recognise the necessity and possibility of at least certain forms of international financial regulation. The BIS in Basel, where the most important countries' central bankers meet each month in order to discuss the state of the world and, where possible, coordinate their policies, adopted a binding rule in 1988 (after protracted negotiations) setting the standard for reserves composition that all internationally active banks must meet. This same BIS, once described as an 'international freemasonry that flourished in Basel',[17] adopted a provisional directive in 1995 that banks can use to calculate the reserves they must have to cover possible losses on the financial markets, including derivatives.

Given the heightened financial instability in the world, these are very modest steps; but they are regulatory measures, which show that regulatory measures are in fact possible. If international regulation is possible, there must be possibilities for national regulation as well. International regulation is harder than national regulation; it requires in any event that transactions be tracked and noted at some subglobal, regional or national level.

Fifth, it is not true that more technology and more internationalisation by definition lead to less control and surveillance. True, that is now the case, but it need not be, even with existing, one-sidedly designed technological means. By applying the new technologies on a larger scale and by means of internationalised financial markets it is in principle all the easier to track and note all financial transactions.[18] The difficulty of doing this is often exaggerated, given that in each sector of the market three or four computer systems at most are used to make deals. The overwhelming majority of currency transactions is carried out with three systems: the business information conglomerate Reuters; Minex, a Japanese company; and EBS, a consortium where the largest banks in the currency markets work together with the electronic information conglomerate Quotron. Reuters has more than 19,000 terminals worldwide and estimates that more than 50 per cent of all currency transactions are carried out on its system alone. Bloomberg monopolises stock trading in a comparable way.[19]

The unavoidable conclusion is that 'financial deregulation was, and is, primarily politically driven'. The question is not whether this trend is irreversible, but how long it can go on:

> In the final analysis regulation depends on the political will to enforce adequate sanctions, so that, given the risk of discovery, the majority of people will observe the law. The fact that such laws can always be technically evaded (by some, for a time) is not an argument against them or their enforcement, any more than the existence of unsolved murders constitutes an argument against the homicide laws.[20]

The global elite itself does not believe entirely in irreversibility, moreover. If it did it would not be so hard at work creating international institutions and agreements that threaten any country that attempts a turnabout with collective punishment. Agreements like the US-Canadian Free Trade Agreement, the North American Free Trade Agreement (NAFTA) and the GATT Uruguay Round are far more than commercial treaties. They are explicit attempts to curtail national sovereignty.[21]

New technological possibilities clearly do play a major role in internationalisation and globalization. They make revolutionary changes possible, and as soon as barriers (legal, social, fiscal or regulatory) to their application are removed or reduced, new applications and possibilities arise through a sort of self-reinforcing processs, as more money and knowledge are invested in them. But this is not an autonomous process that takes place in a vacuum: institutional factors and relationships of forces delimit the playing field. Scholars are increasingly attuned to the tight links that often connect technological innovations to changes in the organisation of production and markets, institutional shifts, and development

of new infrastructure.[22] In this framework the phrase
'enabling technologies' has been coined.[23] Even Marx, who
has often been accused of determinism, portrays 'technology
more as an enabling factor than as an original cause,
autonomous force, or determining factor'.[24]

Enabling technologies allow markets to expand into new
geographical areas. Lower-cost sites can be used only if
distances can be bridged without excessive costs and if such
operations can be effectively coordinated and tracked. The
development of 'enabling technologies' is a precondition for
development of international production and financial flows
and transnational firms. Technologies in the fields of transport, communication and the organising of complex, spread-
out activities are particularly important. But however
important these technologies may be, they cannot be considered the causes of international production or transnational
firms; they only make these phenomena possible.

Towards an Explanation

As if in a caricature of dogmatic Marxist theory, many explanations present globalization as the direct result of revolutionary technological change. But the application of these
technological innovations is only possible thanks to social,
that is economic, political, legal and institutional changes,
nationally as well as internationally. It is interesting, for
example, that the Commission of the European Union gives
high priority to settling every possible legal and institutional
issue and complication properly in its quest to increase
Europe's share in the technological forward march of the
world's peoples. A 'high-level group', including major corporate executives, wrote a recommendation to the Commission
on this subject, recommending among other things protection
of international property rights, preferably on an international
level; more rapid development of electronic and legal safe-
guards; development of new rules on media ownership; and
anti-trust policies adapted to new market conditions.

But why then have the underlying social changes been
occurring? There is no avoiding this question, unless one

supposes that the human race has experienced privatisation, deregulation, technological changes, liberalisation, the disproportionate growth of the financial sector relative to the productive sector, the depoliticisation of political decisions and the extension of the market simply by accident. In that case, there is nothing to explain, and the question why all the changes happened in the early 1980s that made globalization possible has a simple answer: chance. But people who are satisfied with the idea that globalization began through a coincidental convergence of individual decisions, all coincidentally having the same effects, explain nothing at all. What's more, they condemn themselves to reacting to accomplished facts once it is too late, without understanding why.

The following chapters try to answer the question of how the political, social, economic and institutional changes that made globalization possible *can* be understood. The attempt itself may strike some people as strange. In this postmodern age of 'fragmentation' or 'end of ideology', it is rather unfashionable to posit overarching connections and coherence among a variety of social, economic and ideological developments and trends in the world, which are generally presented separately from one other. Not many people at universities or in scholarly journals bother with making these kinds of connections.

But for those who hope to break through the widespread feelings of hopelessness and powerlessness at the apparently uncontrolled, unstoppable wave of globalization, an explanation of why this is happening, what is causing it and where it is heading is of fundamental importance. That in itself is sufficient justification for the search for and discussion of a framework in which radical changes in society, beginning with the economy, can be analysed, explained and understood. We can find solid ground from which to begin by looking at the laws of motion of the capitalist economy.

CHAPTER 3

Long Waves of Capitalist Development

I am in some respects a Marxist. I am for example of the opinion that the economy is primary. Look, De Gaulle said: 'The economy is like the army's food supply: it brings up the rear.' Nonsense. The economy leads, the rest follows: you can immediately see the long-term cultural, political and social consequences of either a flourishing or a withering economy.

Frits Bolkestein, former leader of the right-wing Dutch party VVD, current European Commissioner[1]

In the past, waves and cycles, long, medium and short, had been accepted by businessmen and economists rather as farmers accept the weather, which also has its ups and downs. There was nothing to be done about them: they created opportunities or problems, they could lead to bonanzas or bankruptcy for individuals or industries ...

Eric Hobsbawm[2]

A capitalist economy does not develop evenly. Every day national and international research institutes, economists and analysts try to predict how much economic growth is to be expected, what will happen with inflation and to what extent unemployment will rise or fall. Making these predictions is not easy; sometimes it seems as if the direction the economy is headed is beyond human measurement.[3] The OECD's slip-up in late 1994 – just before the outbreak of the Mexican peso crisis – in forecasting glorious times ahead for the Mexican economy is well known; the OECD made the same mistake again in early 1997 with the 'Asian Tigers' just before their crisis began. The IMF hardly does any better. For example, it predicted in September 1994 that the major industrialised countries would grow by 3.6 per cent in 1995, but had to lower its prediction to 3.0 per cent six months later and to 2.4 per cent after another six months.

Nonetheless, economic developments are not simply random. Nor is there constant, steady forward movement. Phases of growth and stagnation succeed each other in a varying rhythm but with a certain regularity. No economist denies that there are cycles of economic development. These business cycles lasted about ten years when nineteenth-century political economists began to study fluctuations in economic development. Today their length is only four or five years, roughly speaking the average life span of company equipment. These regularly occurring cycles are the result of the economy's internal mechanisms, and are thus endogenous and self-regulating.

As any basic economics textbook mentions, employers aim at making as much profit as possible. Their individual decisions are made in order to maximise their profit rates – the ratio between their profits and their invested constant capital (means of production plus raw materials) and variable capital (wages). It would be a real miracle if all these uncoordinated decisions coincidentally led to balanced economic development. In fact this is not the case, and ups and downs in economic development are the result.

Marx's analysis of capital's laws of motion in *Das Kapital* still seems surprisingly contemporary,[4] but he did not develop a complete theory of crisis. Over the course of time economists identifying themselves as Marxist have developed four basic explanations for economic cycles:[5]

Falling rate of exploitation: Since unemployment declines in expansive phases, the workers' movement is better situated to demand better conditions of labour. For this reason profits fall relative to variable capital (wages).

Disproportionality: Balanced economic growth requires that the demand for different sorts of goods grow in a proportional way. Since individual employers make their own decisions without any coordination, this is rarely the case.

Underconsumption: Because employers try to keep wages as low as possible, a gap opens between productive capacity and effective demand for consumer goods (Department II). This lag in demand has effects in its turn on the demand for means of production (Department I).

Overaccumulation: Increasing investment leads to a lower rate of return on invested capital, since invested constant capital grows more quickly than the rate of exploitation.

In reality, concrete analysis of short-term cycles shows that different combinations of these factors are generally at work. Monocausal explanations seldom do justice to reality.

These short cycles are not the only pattern that is to be found in the economic development of capitalism. There is also a perceptible long-wave movement of approximately 50 years' duration, with an expansive (A) phase and a recessive (B) phase. These waves are usually called Kondratiev waves after the Russian Marxist Nikolai Kondratiev, who directed an institute in Moscow in the 1920s where research on capitalist economic cycles was carried out. Kondratiev, who was banished by Stalin in 1930 to a camp in Siberia where he later died, was not the first to write about long waves.[6] But he was the first to present substantial empirical material that led to an extended discussion.

Although there is considerable empirical evidence for the existence of long waves, the idea is very controversial among economists. Paul Samuelson, one of the godfathers of modern economic theory, once called them 'science fiction'.[7] Ernest Mandel, by contrast, describes a long wave of rising acceptance of the existence of long waves, running at cross-currents to the rhythms of the phenomenon itself.[8]

When Parvus and Van Gelderen began to discuss long waves during the long expansive phase of 1893–1913, they met with almost no response among academic economists. That changed during the long depressive phase between the two world wars, when the works of Kondratiev, Schumpeter and Dupriez led to extensive discussions. During the long postwar expansive phase long-wave theory was once more largely forgotten or rejected out of hand. Mandel was pretty much the lone exception when he predicted in 1964 that the long expansive phase would end in a new depressive phase in the late 1960s or early 1970s. Since the beginning of the depressive phase in the mid-1970s, however, interest in long waves has risen sharply once more. An immense quantity of articles and books has appeared on the topic. In 1976 even the CIA commissioned a report on long waves.[9]

In Table 3.1 the long waves that have occurred since the end of the eighteenth century are divided into expansive and recessive phases. Various researchers use different dates as turning points, depending, for example, on the countries they focus on, but this does not affect the overall picture.

Table 3.1 Long waves since the end of the eighteenth century[10]

	Expansive phase	Recessive phase
1st long wave	1789–1816	1816–48
2nd long wave	1848–73	1873–96
3rd long wave	1896–1919	1919/20–45
4th long wave	1940/45–67/73	1968/73–...

What are these long waves *of*, then? The distinction between expansive and recessive phases is visible particularly in differences in average economic growth rates. This can be seen for the fourth long wave in Table 3.2, which gives the average annual growth rates of per capital GNP for the industrialised countries.[11]

Table 3.2 GNP per capita in the industralised countries

Year	Dollars (1980 prices)	Annual average change (%)	
1950	3,298	–	–
1973	7,396	1950–73	3.6
1989	10,104	1973–89	2.0

These aggregated statistics hide differences among different countries. But as Table 3.3 shows, the long wave movement is an international phenomenon, observable in all capitalist countries.

Table 3.3 Growth of real GNP and ratio of growth in 1983–92 to growth in 1964–73 (%)[12]

	A: 1964–73	B: 1983–92	B/A
West Germany	4.5	2.9	0.64
France	5.3	2.2	0.42
Italy	5.0	2.4	0.48
UK	3.3	2.3	0.69
US	4.0	2.9	0.72
Canada	5.6	2.8	0.50
Japan	9.6	4.0	0.42
Netherlands	5.6	2.4	0.45

Many people have been convinced by the empirical facts that long waves do exist. But opinions as to the theoretical explanation for the phenomenon diverge:

> That good predictions have proved possible on the basis of Kondratiev Long Waves – this is not very common in economics – has convinced many historians that there is something in them, even if we don't know what.[13]

The first round of discussions over the causes of long waves took place between 1920 and 1950. There were four basic approaches:[14]

1. The *capital investment theory*, associated with Kondratiev himself, posits that long waves result from extensive investments in and depreciation of capital goods used over long periods of time, such as railways, canals and factories. During an economic boom over-investment in capital goods takes place, leading to a decline in which superfluous capital is written off. This devaluation of capital gives rise to the possibility of a new boom.

2. The *capitalist crisis theory*, associated with Leon Trotsky, maintains that long waves are a product of the tendential fall in the rate of profit described by the earliest, classical political economists. According to this theory, long waves are above all a sign of an increase in constant capital, and a long recessive phase does not automatically, that is endogenously, lead to a new expansive phase. A watershed of

this kind is the result of exogenous factors – such as the discovery of a new natural resource, an extension of the market or a historical defeat for the workers' movement – with the result that long-term conditions become more favourable for accumulation. The rise in the rate of profit makes a new expansive phase possible, but a new decline inevitably follows.

3. The *innovation theory*, associated with Joseph Schumpeter, posits that long waves are the result of clusters of innovations at specific moments and in specific economic sectors. These clusters of mutually interlinked innovations create a new leading sector in the economy, which grows quickly and leads to a new upturn. During this expansive phase few new radical innovations take place, since investment in existing technology yields good profits. After a time, however, the innovations that opened the expansion bring in declining returns, cooling off the economy and ultimately leading to a decline. In this phase it becomes attractive once more to innovate, but that does not happen from one moment to the next. This is probably the approach with the most support among long-wave theorists.

4. The *war theory*, associated with a group of largely European scholars, including Dupriez, maintains that long waves are the result of – or closely connected to – major wars. The consequences of periodic major wars – particularly inflation – lead to recurring shocks in the world economy and cause long waves. A group of monetarist economists, related in some ways to the war theorists, developed in the discussion's initial stage a parallel theory, in which not war but gold production influences prices. In both theoretical variants long waves are above all a monetary phenomenon. This school has not played any role in the economic discussion since the 1950s, although it has in political and sociological debates.

There is a fundamental difference between the capitalist crisis theory and the other theories as to the type of explanation given for long waves. By contrast with the others, capitalist crisis theory is non-determinist, in the sense that nothing guarantees that a long recessive wave will make way for a new expansive wave.

From 1923 on, Kondratiev and Trotsky carried on a discussion around this central issue. Capital investments were central to Kondratiev's explanation for long waves. Savings accumulated in the recessive phase are concentrated in extensive investments that lead to a new expansive phase. Trotsky criticised the cyclical character of this theory and argued that long waves are specific historic periods of accelerated or slowed-down economic growth in capitalist development. Unlike short economic cycles, according to Trotsky, a new expansive phase does not begin automatically in the long waves as a result of capitalism's internal dynamic. Non-economic factors – 'system shocks' – are necessary for a new expansive phase: acquisition by capitalism of new countries or continents, the discovery of new natural resources, or major events like wars or revolutions.[15]

During the years of postwar expansion interest in the long-wave debate diminished, but after the generalised recession of 1974–75, which marked a turning point in the fourth long wave for all capitalist countries, interest grew once more. The second round of discussion began in the mid-1970s with publications by Ernest Mandel and Walt Rostow. Three research schools grew up, which pursued the approaches of (respectively) Kondratiev, Trotsky and Schumpeter (a non-Marxist, incidentally). The 'capitalist crisis school' was led by the Belgian Trotskyist economist, Ernest Mandel. The Kondratiev-influenced 'capital investment school' was dominated by Jay Forrester and his team of Dynamic System Modellers at the MIT. The Schumpeterian 'innovation school' gathered around Gerhard Mensch in West Germany and Christopher Freeman in England.[16]

The most important difference between the theory as further developed by Mandel[17] and the other long-wave theories is, just as in the first round of discussion a few decades earlier, the question of whether a new expansive phase begins automatically, that is endogenously, or is dependent on exogenous factors. Schumpeter's approach is 'somewhat deterministic, with its emphasis on innovation without a broader linkage to the social and political institutions'.[18] This kind of determinism is alien to Mandel. He says explicitly that there is no parallelism between the essentially endogenous turn from a long expansion to a long depression and the change from a long depression to a long expansion, which is not endogenous and requires external 'system shocks'. According to this theory, the three long upward waves that began in 1849, 1893 and 1940/49 were not the unavoidable result of the depressions that preceded them, but the result of wars, bourgeois revolutions, successful counter-revolutions or a sharp increase in gold production.[19]

Long Waves as Specific Historical Periods

Chapter 2's conclusion was that globalization is not a direct result of technological development; that technological innovations can be applied only when the necessary social relations are in place. It follows that an explanation of the political, social, economic and institutional changes that have made the globalization process possible has to be non-deterministic. One of the existing long wave theories, the capitalist crisis theory, provides such a non-mechanistic explanation. What, according to this theory, are long waves?

> A long wave – one could also speak of a historical period of capitalism or of a productive order – is a period several decades long in which a constellation of institutional forms takes shape and then goes into decline ... : a constellation that regulates the contradictory play of the parameters of accumulation in a lasting way.[20]

The use of the word 'wave' here instead of 'cycle' is no accident. Unlike short cycles, long waves do not begin automatically, dictated by the laws of motion of capitalism. As Table 3.1 shows, they also have varying lengths. The idea that a long upward wave does not arise automatically out of a long downward wave is crucial for this long wave theory, and distinguishes it from the others. In general under capitalism the average rate of profit is in decline. But three times in history a sharp increase in the rate of profit occurred: after 1848; after 1893; and about 1940 in the US and about 1948–49 in Western Europe and Japan. Each time extra-economic system shocks played a key role, causing a sudden expansion of the world market and a sudden fundamental change in the general conditions of capital accumulation. After 1848 a long-term rise in the rate of profit was made possible by the liberal or bourgeois revolutions in Europe and the discovery of the California gold fields in the wake of the US conquest of half of Mexico in 1846–48. A drastic rise in investments in newly conquered African and Asian colonies and the discovery of the Rand gold fields in South Africa were crucial for rising profit rates after 1893. And the postwar expansive period would never have been possible without the cumulative long-term effects of fascism and war.[21]

For the theoretical background we must go back to Marx. In volume 3 of *Capital* he explains why the average rate of profit tends to fall in a capitalist economy.[22] If we assume that there is in fact such a tendential fall – and all the classical political economists took it for granted – then the key question is whether it is possible to explain long-term increases of the average rate of profit at specific historical turning points.[23] This is indeed possible if we recognise that different key variables in the Marxist 'system' are partially autonomous, that is, that there are no mechanical correlations among them.[24]

Let us specifically examine the rate of profit. According to Marx, its main determinants are fluctuations in the organic composition of capital (c/v), fluctuations in the rate of exploitation (s/v) and fluctuations in capital's turnover time.[25] It follows that a sharp increase in the rate of exploitation, a sharp slowdown in the rate of growth of the organic composition of capital, an acceleration of the turnover time of capital, or a combination of these factors can lead to a rise in the average rate of profit.

Marx also indicates that forces are at work that counteract the tendential fall in the rate of profit. In addition to four different factors (more intense exploitation, reduction of wages, relative surplus population – unemployment – and a cheapening of elements of constant capital) that correspond to the determinants of the rate of profit that have just been mentioned, these forces are: the possibility of an increase in the *quantity* of surplus-value and – more importantly – a flow of capital into countries and sectors where the average organic composition of capital is considerably lower than in the main industrial sectors of the industrialised capitalist countries.

If a number of these factors are simultaneously at work and in this way overcome the long-term decline in the average rate of profit, the average rate of profit increases sharply. The normal, conjunctural, cylical up-and-down movement of the average rate of profit is not eliminated but, as long as the counteracting forces are stronger and more synchronised than before, they act as a brake on the cylical downturns. Expansive long waves are precisely those periods in which the forces that counteract the tendential fall of the rate of profit are forcefully at work in a synchronised way. Depressive long waves, by contrast, are periods in which these forces act less forcefully and are less synchronised.

This all implies that only concrete historical analyses can tell us what factors are responsible for turning points at which new expansive phases in the development of capitalism become possible.

Not the laws of motion of capitalism but the results of the class struggle of a whole historical period are deciding this turning point. What we assume here is a *dialectic of the objective and subjective factors of historical development,* in which the subjective factors are characterized by *relative autonomy*; that is, they are not predetermined directly and unavoidably by what occurred previously in regard to the basic trends of capital accumulation, the trends in transformation of technology, or the impact of these trends on the process of labor organization itself.[26]

Long waves are cut across by the short cycles discussed earlier. These short cycles have a varying average amplitude, depending on the phase of the long wave in which we find ourselves, with the conjunctural highs being lower and the lows deeper in a recessive phase. Every long wave is characterised by a 'dominant mode of functioning' of capitalism, a 'productive order', with four significant levels:[27]

1. *Mode of accumulation,* including: competitive relationships (industrial and financial structure, extent of monopolies in the economy, relationship between banking and industrial

capital, modalities of state intervention in the economy) and the relationships between capital and labour (organisation of labour, wage structure – is there a minimum wage, are there collective bargaining agreements? – and the working class's type of consumption).

2. *Material forces of production,* in which innovations play an important role. Mandel says that long depressive waves are generally characterised by a multiplication of inventions and technological innovations, which essentially remain experimental. This seems to have changed somewhat since the early 1980s, given that much new technology is already being applied, though without restoring labour productivity growth to levels comparable to the postwar expansive phase.

3. *Organisation of social relations,* that is, the (para-)state institutions that structure and organise reproduction, 'social peace', and the workforce's subordination to the ruling order: the system of political representation, the educational system (important in the 'production' of the labour force), the right to work, a social security system and the maintenance of order.

4. An *international division of labour,* including: the hierarchical order of military and political power, the place of different economies in the productive process (who supplies the raw materials, who produces the most sophisticated industrial products?), the international role of currencies (is there a generally accepted international reserve currency?) and the direction in which international financial flows go.

Summing up, we can see that long waves are far more than just rises and declines in the capitalist economy's growth rates. They are specific historical periods, differing historical realities, with distinctive characteristics:

> The Marxist explanation of these long waves, with its peculiar interweaving of internal economic factors, exogenous 'environmental' changes, and their mediation through sociopolitical developments (i.e., periodic changes in the overall balance of class forces and intercapitalist relationship of forces, the outcomes of momentous class struggles and of wars) gives this historical reality of the long wave an integrated 'total' character.[28]

In the following section and in Chapter 4 we discuss the postwar expansive phase and the developments since the 1974/75 turnaround within this theoretical framework.

The Postwar Expansion ...

The postwar period up until the mid-1970s has been called capitalism's Golden Age. The first quarter-century after the Second World War saw the rise of a series of developed capitalist welfare states. Social and collective services were expanded, subsidies for education, culture, housing and health care went up, buying power rose steadily and unemployment was low. These were years of strong economic growth and active economic management by governments: 'We are all Keynesians now,' said US President Nixon in 1971.[29]

Both inside the academic community and among economic advisers and policymakers, optimism about growth and belief in full employment and technological progress were in their heyday. The idea was widespread among politicians and economists that capitalism had gone through a qualitative change and that the time of crises was gone for good. The future French minister, Stoleru, wrote in 1970,

> It has often been said that a crisis like the Great Depression could not happen today, given the progress that has been made in techniques of state countercyclical intervention. These claims, however presumptuous they may seem, are not without foundation.[30]

Not only for industrialised countries but also in many of the world's poor countries, the first postwar decades were a time of progress. Hobsbawm recalls that there were no major famines during the Golden Age, except as a result of wars and 'political madness, as in China'.[31] The world population multiplied several times over, yet at the same time life expectancy increased by an average of 17 years between the late 1930s and late 1960s. Food production increased faster than population not only in the developed countries, but also in the non-industrialised world. In every region of the Third

World except Latin America food production per person grew by over 1 per cent a year in the 1950s. This growth in food production continued into the 1960s, although much more slowly, while production in general took off. Many developing countries experienced growth rates that were unprecedented in the history of the world economy. In 42 developing countries – including twelve in South America, six in the Middle East and North Africa, and as many as 15 in sub-Saharan Africa – the economy grew each year by more than 2.5 per cent per capita at least from 1960 up until the first oil crisis. In only ten countries for which statistics are available did per capita income not rise in these years.[32]

What made this Golden Age possible? As Tables 3.4 and 3.5 show, the economy was growing quickly and productivity was rising rapidly. The main factors underlying this growth can be summed up schematically in a number of points:[33]

- An extensive renewal of the stock of capital goods after the great depression of the 1930s and the Second World War.
- Enormous quantities of cheap labour, which meant a major increase in the rate of exploitation. This was particularly the case in Germany, Japan, France, Italy, etc., where the working class had experienced severe defeats by fascism and in war, and to a certain extent also in the US, where the trade union bureaucracy gave up the strike weapon during the Second World War.
- Large quantities of cheap raw materials from Third World countries.
- Clusters of technological and organisational innovations, with major consequences for productivity growth and consumer demand. This wave was characterised among other things by the fact that, following the mechanical production of industrial consumer goods (since the early nineteenth century) and the mechanical production of machines (since the mid-nineteenth century), raw materials and food products also began to be mechanically processed. For the first time all branches of the economy were industrialised.[34]
- Permanent military reflation[35] through the Korean War and Cold War.

Table 3.4 Annual average economic growth in different periods,
1820–1973 (weighted average of 16 countries) (%)[36]

Period	GNP growth	GNP per capita growth
1820–1870	2.2	1.0
1870–1913	2.5	1.4
1913–1950	1.9	1.2
1950–1973	4.9	3.8

Table 3.5 Productivity increase per employee per year (1870–1973)
(%)[37]

		1870–1950	1950–73
France	Agriculture	1.4	5.6
	Industry	1.4	5.2
	Services	0.7	3.0
Germany	Agriculture	0.2	6.3
	Industry	1.3	5.6
	Services	0.7	3.0
Japan	Agriculture	0.7	7.3
	Industry	1.7	9.5
	Services	0.5	3.6
UK	Agriculture	1.4	4.7
	Industry	1.2	2.9
	Services	0.2	1.6
US	Agriculture	1.3	5.5
	Industry	1.6	2.4
	Services	1.1	1.8

As we saw in the previous section, according to Marxist
theory the beginning of a long expansive phase of the long
waves depends on a drastic increase in the rate of profit. The
explanation for a sharp increase in the rate of profit that made
it possible for capitalism to escape from the long period of
relative stagnation between 1914 and 1939, for example, was
the historic defeat suffered by the working class in the 1930s
and 1940s. In Germany, Japan, Italy, France and Spain the
increase in the rate of exploitation was gigantic: between 100

and 300 per cent. Together with a slowdown in the rate of growth of the organic composition of capital and an acceleration of capital turnover time, this increase in the rate of exploitation explains the sudden rise in the average rate of profit, which was followed by a sharp increase in capital accumulation. The possibility of investing capital in the arms industry, with government-guaranteed profits, also played a role.[38]

After a turning point is reached in economic development, and the resultant new long expansive wave, dynamic processes are set in motion. Technological developments, the situation of the working class (level of wages, extent of unemployment, organisation) and economic, political, social and institutional conditions more generally play a crucial role. The specific character of the welfare state in Western Europe, for example, can only be understood against the backdrop of the 'Communist threat', that is in the light of postwar developments in Eastern Europe and the pre-revolutionary situations that existed or threatened to arise at the end of the war, particularly in France, Italy and Greece.

A productive order arose in the postwar years with a concrete, coherent combination of the four levels listed in the last section. Summed up in a few key terms, the postwar expansive phase rested on four pillars:[39]

1. *Taylorism:* A scientific organisation of labour with an unprecedented intensification of rhythms of work, with as one major result a steady increase in labour productivity.

2. *Fordism:* Forty per cent of the economic growth in the Golden Age was related to automobile production and housing.[40] In retrospect, as Keynes had predicted, including wage earners in the dynamic of consumer markets turned out to be the best medicine for traditional crises of overproduction, as long as mass consumption did not increase more quickly than productivity and did not interfere with profits.

3. *Keynesianism:* In place of laissez-faire liberalism, active state intervention in the economy by means of automatic stabilisers (such as, for example, the social security system) and with budgetary and monetary policy in order to prevent destabilising stock exchange crashes and recessions.

4. *US hegemony:* Expressed at Bretton Woods, where the dollar acquired the status of international reserve currency. The Bretton Woods system did not arise spontaneously but was prepared during the course of the war.

Neither technological changes and organisational innovations nor Keynesian policies were in themselves sufficient to establish the fundamental postwar changes in the regulation of capitalism. All this, plus the Pax Americana, debt expansion, oligopolistic competition and the Fordist compromise between labour and capital, were necessary.[41]

In Western Europe the welfare state quickly took shape as a result of a 'social compromise' among employers, trade unions and the state. It was the outcome of strategic cooperation by labour and capital within the postwar institutional framework. This so-called 'historic compromise' led among other things to a considerable extension of the social security system. 'Employers promised to commit themselves to the creation of adequate employment for the greatest possible number of male workers, while employee organisations gave up their traditional demand for socialisation of production and accepted the employers' right to manage.'[42] The state took on an active role in the fields of macroeconomic policy, labour relations and extension and organisation of social services.

The trade union movement played an essential role in this whole process. In return for recognition and centralised bargaining, union leaders accepted that employers would continue to call the shots and made sure that radical workers were held on a short leash. In the Netherlands, for example, the Foundation for Labour, which was set up immediately after the war, played an important role in this process. On the one hand it kept the unions in check and made them share responsibility for the system by incorporating their leaders into forms of class collaboration; on the other hand it isolated and marginalised the militant trade unionists, who were organised in the Communist-led United Trades Federation (EVC). Stikker, an employer and central figure in the creation of the Foundation for Labour, was utterly afraid that Allied victory in the war would give rise to economic yearnings among the population that would be impossible to satisfy in the short run, and his fear was that disillusionment would make the masses ripe for revolutionary ideas. Stikker considered the infection of such ideas, 'the isms that promise mountains of gold', the greatest danger for the period immediately after the war. He therefore urged the creation of as many jobs as possible as quickly as possible: 'the masses must be gotten off the streets, they must work, there must be peace and quiet, whatever it costs!'[43]

Splits in trade union movements in the US, France, Italy and other countries, as well as in the World Federation of Trade Unions, were the outcome of conscious efforts by figures who thought much as Stikker did and had the backing of US policymakers, funds and intelligence services. As a result, there was a 'compromise' in which both employers and unions made concessions in return for a degree of moderation from the other side and agreed to accept an active role for the state.

The rise of the welfare state was another outcome of this compromise. The power of the labour movement and its organisations, the social democratic parties and unions, was not the only cause of the rise of the welfare state: welfare states also developed in Western European countries where Christian Democratic parties were in power. This had consequences for the kind of welfare states that emerged. They remained largely reactive in character, directed above all at organising income transfers. They were not meant to 'have the ability to influence the structural parameters of socioeconomic and labour market relationships in any essential way'.[44]

... and Its End

In the mid-1970s – earlier in some countries, later in others – an end came to the expansive period thoroughout the capitalist world. This turnaround was completely unexpected for most economists and politicians. It took some time for people to be convinced that something fundamental really had changed. As late as 1972 the UN had written in a report on the European economies that there was no reason to doubt that the under-lying growth trend of the 1960s would continue throughout the 1970s. The OECD projected in the early 1970s that growth would continue in the middle term at about 5 per cent a year.[45] That turned out not to be the case. As Tables 3.6, 3.7 and 3.8 show, economic growth declined, annual productivity increases went down and unemployment rose.

Table 3.6 Average annual growth of real GNP in six major industrialised countries (%)[46]

	1950–73	1973–79	1979–83
US	2.2	1.9	0.7
UK	2.5	1.3	0.4
France	4.1	2.6	1.1
Germany	5.0	2.6	0.5
Italy	4.8	2.0	0.6
Japan	8.4	3.0	3.9

Table 3.7 Productivity increase per employee per year (1950–81) (%)[47]

		1950–73	1973–81
France	Agriculture	5.6	3.5
	Industry	5.2	3.2
	Services	3.0	1.6
Germany	Agriculture	6.3	3.9
	Industry	5.6	2.6
	Services	3.0	1.6
Japan	Agriculture	7.3	1.1
	Industry	9.5	4.7
	Services	3.6	1.9
UK	Agriculture	4.7	2.8
	Industry	2.9	1.8
	Services	1.6	0.7
US	Agriculture	5.5	1.6
	Industry	2.4	-0.2
	Services	1.8	0.1

Table 3.8 Average unemployment (1952–83) (%)[48]

	1952–64	1965–73	1973–79	1980–83
US	5.0	4.5	6.5	8.4
UK	2.5	3.2	4.6	9.0
France	1.7	2.4	4.2	7.6
Germany	2.7	0.8	3.1	5.7
Italy	5.9	3.4	6.0	8.6
Japan	1.9	1.3	1.8	2.3

All these changes had major consequences. Economic expansion had created the material conditions for steadily rising living standards and low unemployment and, for the whole edifice of the welfare state, enabling social and collective services to be substantially expanded in the postwar years. With the turn from an expansive to a depressive long wave, it was no longer possible to guarantee almost full employment, expand the social security system, give real annual wage increases to the employed or reduce poverty. Bringing the reduced rate of profit back up again became the employers' top priority, with attacks on working conditions and living standards and on the gains of the welfare state as a result.

Why did the postwar expansive phase come to an end? Generally speaking, because the special conditions that had made the Golden Age possible came to an end, and because the period of expansion led to new contradictions: increased competition among the developed capitalist countries, leading among other things to the collapse of the Bretton Woods system; rising inflation in a context of more militant trade unions under conditions of almost full employment; fiscal crises accompanying reforms of the welfare state; and rising prices for raw materials from the Third World, expressed among other ways in the 1973 'oil crisis'.[49]

To grasp the underlying mechanisms we must return to long-wave theory. Mandel observes that international capitalist expansion after the Second World War was borne on a wave of debt. Rising inflation was the result, but ultimately it was not enough to smooth over capitalism's contradictions. He lists the eight factors given below as leading jointly to the end of the postwar expansion and the beginning of another period of capitalism.[50]

1. During the whole postwar expansive long wave, there was a steady rise of the organic composition of capital and a consequent fall in the rate of profit.[51]

2. The specific circumstances of the beginning of the technological revolution and of new industrial sectors that developed because of it – and the excess profits that they guaranteed for leading firms – gradually disappeared as the technological revolution was generalised.

3. It became more difficult to achieve new increases in capital's turnover time. A revolution continued in the telecommunications sector, but further progress in sectors such as transport, sales of goods and turnover of liquid holdings was very limited in the late 1960s and 1970s.

4. The long period of rapid growth created the conditions for a growing disproportionality between the rate of growth of production capacity for capital and consumer goods and the rate of growth in the raw materials sector, which is more directly linked to natural circumstances and therefore less flexible. As a result, it was impossible for the relative decline of raw materials prices, which had been going on for almost 20 years (1952–71), to continue. The 1973 'oil crisis' was an example. A positive effect of this turn of events was that it stimulated the search for alternative materials and energy sources. It brought the productivist, polluting character of capitalism more to light, along with the need to use raw materials and energy more sparingly and tackle waste and pollution at their sources.

5. During the whole expansive long wave a potential capacity for overproduction was built up, because productive capacity grew more quickly than consumer buying power.

6. Given the factors mentioned, an erosion of profitability could only be prevented through an ongoing, substantial increase in the rate of exploitation. That was certainly achieved in the first phase of the expansive long wave, but became steadily more difficult because technological changes lost their momentum and a situation of almost full employment arose. Just at the moment that the increase in organic composition accelerated, the rise in the rate of exploitation levelled off. This made a fall in the rate of profit unavoidable.

7. In a situation of increasing difficulties of realisation[52] and declining profitability, inflation could only fulfil its

function of putting off the day of reckoning as long as it rose higher and higher in each successive cycle. But in practice as well as in theory, after a certain point a permanent rise in inflation turned out to be counterproductive for economic expansion. This was the case among other reasons because of the snowball effect of anticipatatory wage and price hikes, the negative real rate of interest, and the fact that long-term rates of returns became harder to calculate.

8. The permanent growth of multinationals increasingly undermined the effectiveness of state economic intervention. Combining these last two factors – a different inflation rate in each country and the declining ability of nation-states' to deal with multinationals – helps us understand why the Bretton Woods monetary system collapsed, leading to increasing international monetary anarchy.

Summing up, we can understand global economic developments since the Second World War with the help of Marxist long-wave theory. Since each long wave is characterised by an entirely distinctive constellation of a mode of accumulation, material forces of production, a way of organising social relationships and an international division of labour, every facet of the postwar productive order came under material and ideological pressure once the economy turned around in the mid-1970s. Nothing worked automatically any more. This set an extensive, far-reaching process of economic, social, political and institutional change in motion, including, as we will see, the process that later became known as globalization.

CHAPTER 4

Stagnation and Restructuring: Towards a New Expansion?

We used to read predictions that by 2000 everyone would work 30–hour weeks, and the rest would be leisure. But as we approach 2000 it seems more likely that half of us will be working 60–hour weeks and the rest of us will be unemployed.

William Bridges[1]

In 1974–75, a recession hit all the world's major countries, the first instance of its kind since the Second World War. This was for politicians and economists a bolt from the blue. The reigning consensus had been that capitalism had gone through a qualitative change and would ensure growth, prosperity and full employment for the indefinite future. Walter Heller, former chairperson of Kennedy's Council of Economic Advisers, predicted in 1967 that the economy would expand even more rapidly in the future, with fewer ups and downs than in the 1950s. German professors Wilhelm Weber and Hubert Weiss said in that same year that 'there are no more crises in the old sense' and that even deep recessions had become 'atypical'. The well-known British economist Roy Harrod wrote in 1969 that full employment could be considered a permanent feature of the British economy.[2]

The Turnaround and Its Consequences

But the first postwar generalised recession was, as we saw in Chapter 3, the beginning of a qualitatively different period. Economic growth continued to decline and profits fell (see

Table 4.1) while unemployment rose sharply, to almost 17 million in 1975–76 in the OECD countries.[3]

Table 4.1 Development of profits and GNP in seven industrialised countries (France, Germany, Italy, Japan, Spain, UK and US) (%)[4]

Year	Rate of profit	Moving average rate of GNP growth
1965	22.4	4.0
1966	22.5	4.0
1967	22.1	4.3
1968	22.3	4.6
1969	21.5	5.0
1970	20.3	5.2
1971	20.2	5.1
1972	20.0	4.9
1973	19.8	5.1
1974	17.3	4.5
1975	16.4	3.6
1976	16.8	3.7
1977	17.0	3.8
1978	17.2	4.0
1979	16.5	3.6
1980	15.2	3.0
1981	15.1	3.0
1982	14.3	3.0

Politicians' and economists' reaction to this turnaround was at first 'business as usual'. They tried to reverse the fall in economic growth rates and profits with traditional Keynesian policies of demand stimulation and an extension of credits to employers, households and Third World countries. In July 1978 a summit of the leaders of the major industrialised nations took place in Bonn. US President Jimmy Carter had been putting pressure on European governments for some time to pull their stagnating economies out of the dip with more government spending. The idea was that increased growth in Europe would lift the whole world economy, and among other things would improve the US balance of payments. The powerful German economy was supposed to be the locomotive; Chancellor Helmut Schmidt agreed at the conference to increase the German budget deficit. An internationally coordinated Keynesian fiscal stimulus was supposed to turn the economic tide. But its main result was rising inflation. One country after another (Thatcher in England, Barre in France) pulled back from the commitment it had made in Bonn.[5]

Why were the first reactions to the situation so routine? To begin with, as already mentioned, the timing and character of the recession took politicians and economists completely by surprise. It is therefore not so strange that its depth was not immediately evident after almost 30 years of prosperity, and that the first reactions were the ones that had become usual in the postwar period. Shell chief executive Wagner, who wrote a harsh letter in 1976 to the left-of-centre Dutch government under Joop den Uyl to demand more pro-business policies, observed, looking back 20 years later, that the Netherlands had simply not been ready for a message of that kind:

> The Golden Sixties – with industrialisation, full employment and an overheated labour market – were gone. Nonetheless the expansion of the welfare state continued. The Netherlands was trapped in automatic mechanisms such as indexing. Two external shocks, the 1973 and '79 oil crises, were still not enough to shift the 'consensus economy' in another direction. Nobody could see it, people just weren't ripe for it.[6]

There was another contributing, interrelated factor: European employees, trade unions and much of the left were (still) not willing to accept drastic austerity measures. The unions were strong and, at least compared with today, radical. The Dutch Industrial Union for example was still calling for fundamental social change, and a leader of the Dutch Catholic Trades Union made history by attacking the elite '200 rich' who dominated the economy. Stagnant productivity in the 1970s definitely cannot be attributed to technological factors alone: the strength of the unions and workers and the radicalism of the most militant workers in much of Europe acted as a brake on social and political pressures to increase the pace of work. Almost full employment enabled workers to make more demands, and employees in a series of

countries, industries and companies used their power to
control the pace of work, working hours and working conditions. 'For capital, the skill of the workers turned from being
a necessary condition for industrial development into being an
obstacle to capital accumulation.'[7]

More generally, much of the world was affected by a deep
social crisis in the late 1960s: the Vietnam war and massive
mobilisations against it; May 1968 in France and the Italian
'hot autumn' of 1969; the bloody repression of the Mexican
student revolt in 1968; youth revolts against authority, alien-
ation, exploitation and oppression and for profound democratisation; the virtual revolutions against dictatorships in
Portugal (1974–75) and Spain (1975); and mass radicalisa-
tion of women in the second wave of feminism. In this
context, a sudden, sharp change of course in economic policy,
including cuts in social and public services and an end to
annual wage increases, would have been impossible; it could
have led to politically explosive situations. In the 1970s, for
example, employers would never have been able to push
through the far-reaching forms of flexibility that exist in
companies today.[8] Policies were aimed rather at softening or
postponing recessions. But the price was rising inflation and
increasing budget deficits.

This situation could not continue for long. From the late
1970s on, the fight against inflation was proclaimed to be the
top priority for monetary policy. On 6 October 1979 the new
chairman of the US Federal Reserve, monetarist Paul
Volcker, announced that it would drastically restrict the
money supply in order to curb rapidly accelerating inflation.[9]
Never before had the Federal Reserve contracted the money
supply so much so quickly. Since, to the surprise of Volcker
and his colleagues, inflation remained high, the Federal
Reserve raised interest rates more, to almost 20 per cent.[10]
Other central banks followed suit. Since that time fighting
inflation has remained the number one priority of virtually
every central bank. Although no economist can explain what
is so disastrous about a few per cent inflation, maintenance of
price stability – that is, a rate of inflation between 0 and 2 per
cent – trumps any other concern for national central bankers,
and since 1999 for the European Central Bank.[11]

The result of central bankers' restrictive monetary policies was a second generalised recession in 1980–82, a deeper recession than the previous one. Growth declined further, profits continued to decline (see Table 4.1) and unemployment rose dramatically, to almost 30 million in the OECD countries.[12] For many Third World countries the 1980–82 recession marked the real beginning of their troubles. As inflation declined, real interest rates skyrocketed on loans that they had obtained on easy terms.[13] At the same time their possibilities for economic growth declined drastically as a result of the new recession. The result was the debt crisis. In 1982 Mexico was the first to announce that it could not meet the payments on its foreign debt, and other countries followed.[14]

As the effects of mass unemployment began to take hold, European employers gradually managed to rein in the power of the unions and radical workers and shift the relationship of forces between capital and labour. In many European countries the turning point came in the early 1980s, when unemployment rose rapidly and several major conglomerates went under. In the words of former Shell chief executive Wagner, 'At last everyone was ready to recognise the market as the stern disciplinarian of the social order.'[15]

As the postwar expansion came to an end and the economic tide turned, every aspect of the postwar productive order came under pressure and into question. Rapidly increasing unemployment and harder competition among the major capitalist countries played a crucial role. The huge increase in unemployment had an impact above all on the second and third levels of the productive order laid out in Chapter 3: the mode of accumulation and the mode of organisation of social relations. In times of almost full employment, wage earners are in a position of strength; improvements can be won more easily and the threat of worsening conditions is easier to ward off. A rise in unemployment leads to a weaker union movement, which gives employers the nerve to take the offensive and begin to undermine wage earners' rights and past gains. 'One could hardly ask for a clearer confirmation of the analysis Marx made in *Das Kapital* over a century ago: in the long term capitalism cannot survive without an industrial reserve army, that is without unemployment.'[16]

Rapidly rising unemployment was used, as in earlier
periods of history, to impose lower wages and more work on
those who had not (yet) lost their jobs. Employers began to
reorganise the labour process in their companies; they
imposed more and more flexibility in working time and conditions, permanent restructuring, and contracting out of work
that was not part of their 'core business'.[17]

As soon as the expansive phase was over, 'national compromises' with unions and governments, which until then had
been relatively advantageous for capital, began to be an
obstacle to the 'cleansing process' needed to raise the rate of
profit once more. There was less financial room for concessions to wage earners, while there was less need for such
concessions as a result of the changed relationship of forces
between capital and labour.

The fact that expansion had shrunk the industrial reserve
army was a major reason why capitalism's years of prosperity
had come to an end. The rate of exploitation had stopped rising
and in fact had begun to decline from its high level. The tight
labour market had strengthened the position of wage earners; in
such a situation a period of somewhat slower growth is unavoidable unless the employers succeed in breaking employees' resistance and achieving a new, sharp increase in the rate of
exploitation. Since that cannot happen without freezing or even
lowering real wages, capital in the second half of the 1970s
launched a period of more intense class struggle. As part of its
offensive, it consciously used the maintenance and expansion of
the industrial reserve army as a tool of economic policy.

The postwar 'agreement' was, as it were, unilaterally abro-
gated. A prolonged period of guerrilla warfare began between
unions and 'the politicians', with far-reaching liberalisation,
deregulation, privatisation, and dismantling of social security
and the public sector as war aims.[18] This made the 1980s the
time of the 'crisis of the welfare state':[19] a welfare state that
society could no longer afford, according to a growing army of
employers, politicians and economists, that put a premium on
laziness and inactivity and therefore had to be cut back. A
start was made with major reductions in social spending.

Naturally, these developments did not escape economists'
attention. Many of them around the world came to the

conclusion that Keynesian policies – active, countercyclical state interventions and full employment – no longer worked and urgently needed to be replaced by a monetarist policy geared at maintaining price stability. 'Liberalisation', 'more competition' and 'more market' are the core concepts of the new paradigm that became hegemonic in political science and economics.[20] But it was not economists' theories that changed reality; they simply gave a sense of coherence and direction to political forces with deep social roots.[21] The ideological changes that occurred are a good illustration of the fact that long waves are specific historical periods with an all-encompassing character. Changes in economic theory can be seen in this light as an expression of the changed relationship of forces between labour and capital.[22]

At the same time, major changes took place on the fourth level of the productive order, that is, in the international division of labour. Up until the early 1970s the US was the world's dominant economic, military and political power, but its position came under pressure when Japan and Western Europe rebuilt their economies and as international competition intensified because of economic stagnation. In Chapter 2 we saw that the Bretton Woods framework collapsed in the early 1970s. This not only meant the end of a more or less stable international monetary system, in which exchange rates could only be changed in exceptional circumstances; a second element of the Bretton Woods system also disappeared.

In reaction to the protectionism of the 1930s, the postwar international system was geared mainly towards expanding trade. In order to maintain the fixed exchange rates that were considered necessary for this purpose, national economies were sheltered to a certain extent from the rest of the world. The existence of fixed exchange rates protected currencies from short-term monetary fluctuations on the world market. At the same time, countries kept a number of tools available to regulate international capital flows to a certain extent through controls on cross-border capital transactions. Keeping these tools in reserve was a major element of the Keynesian conception of the active, interventionist state.[23] The end of the Bretton Woods system also knocked these policy instruments out of the hands of states, as governments opened the door wide for an immense increase in international capital flows – Thatcher came to power in 1979, Reagan in 1980, and the Dutch Christian Democrat Lubbers and the German Kohl not long afterwards – and all their destabilising consequences.

Finally, there was of course another fundamental change in the world that had major consequences for the evolution of capitalism. The fall of the Berlin Wall and ensuing collapse of the bureaucratic regimes in Eastern Europe and the Soviet Union in the early 1990s rapidly opened up an extensive area, until then closed off, with new prospects for investment, trade, production and sales. Kohl and Mitterand's initiative to speed up European integration, which led to the Maastricht Treaty, was one response to these developments.

The fall of the Wall not only led to the introduction of capitalist relations of production in a steadily growing area of Eastern Europe and the former Soviet Union; the neoliberal tidal wave that swept across the world and successfully opened more and more Third World countries to investment, speculation and exports could spread unhindered because there was no longer any alternative to the IMF, the World Bank and the financial markets. The support that the Soviet Union used to give to Third World countries was not charity but a means of preserving its own sphere of influence, and thus came with political strings attached. But for many countries it was better than nothing. Many of them, like Cuba, lost an ally, a major trading partner and an economic patron almost overnight when the USSR collapsed. Francis Fukuyama expressed the *Zeitgeist* with his declaration that the end of history had arrived.[24] The ideological message was clear: in the new world order capitalism had definitely triumphed, and there was no escaping it.

We can see now how economic globalization became an important element of the restructuring that began to gather steam in all capitalist countries from the early 1980s on. When an end came to postwar prosperity in the mid-1970s, policymakers resisted a return to the protectionism and separate monetary blocs of the 1930s. The still vivid memories of the interwar years – and even more the 30-year-long expansion of international trade, the consequent interdependence of national economies and the increased weight of multinationals – made a further acceleration of internationalisation possible and probable.

By decreasing their dependence on their 'home countries' and playing different countries' workers, unions and governments off against one another, multinational companies, investors and speculators were able to generate much more pressure on all fronts than had been possible in a single country. They could obtain lower tax rates – 'or else we'll move abroad' – more subsidies – 'or else we'll move abroad' – lower direct and indirect wage costs for the same or more work – 'or else we'll move abroad' – less say by unions or government in what happened in the company – 'or else we'll move abroad' – less stringent environmental rules – 'other countries don't make so much fuss' – fewer restrictions as to what products can be sold in what countries – 'unless we sell more our competitors will bury us' – and fewer rules and demands that affect the functioning of the labour market – 'in the US they do fine without all these rules'. All these factors contribute substantially to increasing the rate of profit.

Internationalisation is not a new thing under capitalism, and multinationals have been around for a while. But now a qualitatively more far-reaching step was taken, taking advantage of the relationship of forces changed by the crisis and of the potential of new technologies that had never before been introduced on a large scale. This was most visible in the revolution that took place in the financial sector. The globalization of financial markets has not only made it easier to put countries and governments under pressure and to discipline them; it has also made it easier to send the extensive profits, which thanks to overaccumulation can only partially be productively invested, around the world in search of the highest possible returns. The result is a far-reaching financialisation of the economy and the previously mentioned mushrooming of speculative financial flows.

Globalization – the penetration and transcendence of national frameworks – has become an important element in the process of capitalist restructuring, which has been under way since the early 1980s as a reaction to stagnating growth and the falling rate of profit in the previous period. From the moment that the postwar expansive period came to an end, employers began to experience the national frameworks and compromises that they had been able to live with or even benefit from for several decades as more and more constraining. In order to attain new possibilities for growth and profit, they needed to extend their unbridled search for higher profits, cheaper inputs (particularly raw materials and labour) and new markets on a global scale. The steadily increasing power, influence and size of the multinationals is being brought to bear more and more in order to rid themselves of restrictions on internationalisation and put pressure on governments to soften rules and eliminate obstacles to cross-border capital movements. Big banks in London and the US are exerting steady pressure to win further liberalisation and deregulation of the financial sector.[25] Swedish multinationals like Ikea and Tetrapac, 'products of the Swedish welfare model', have behaved like 'ungrateful internationalists. Swedish capital, liberated from all legal restrictions, is moving out of Sweden to get closer to foreign markets or simply to find cheaper labour'.[26]

Large companies and financial institutions are taking advantage of new technological developments to profit from the greater manoeuvring room that has arisen as a result of liberalisation of financial markets and from the weakening of the union movement by massive unemployment. They are investing, speculating, producing, selling, and buying parts and semi-finished products worldwide ('global sourcing'). They are playing workers off against each other. This is a shift from an 'international economy to a true world economy. This interpenetration destroys the effectiveness of traditional national policies and turns the whole system over to the dictates of the world market – including its mistakes.'[27]

The current trend towards increasing globalization is the product of two interlinked but distinct processes. The first can be characterised as a long-term development in capitalism since about 1870 towards uninterrupted accumulation and increasing international concentration and centralisation of capital.[28] The second consists of the policies of liberalisation, privatisation, deregulation and dismantling of social and democratic gains that have taken shape since the early

1980s.[29] Taken together, these two processes have set a globalization in motion that has its own dynamic, that pushes
relentlessly onwards and that no one and nothing seems to
have under control.

It is no accident that in this time, when the world seems
more complex and less comprehensible than ever, many
people's belief in the possibility of social change has crumbled
or even vanished. New possibilities (lower wages in Asia), new
political taboos (on economic 'fine-tuning' by national
governments and on countercyclical automatic stabilisers)
and new institutional arrangements (independent central
banks and liberalised capital markets) are leading to more and
more new problems (the collapse of one currency after
another), new responses (an acceleration of European
economic integration in order to shore up the competitive
position of European businesses) and new initiatives (the
extension of free-trade zones and customs unions). As a
result, all the pillars of the postwar productive order
mentioned in the previous chapter are changing in major
ways:

1. *Taylorism:* Talk about 'the end of Taylorism'[30] is only
partially justified. New 'Toyotist' management techniques,
with their greater emphasis on teamwork, while widespread,
are far from being universally applied; there are sectors where
hierarchical management and a rigid division of labour are
advancing.[31] But in general the application of new communications technology and new management techniques in the
most important companies and institutions has major consequences for the organising of labour, employees' position and
the functioning and situation of labour organisations.[32]

2. *Fordism:* The 'end of Fordism' and the establishment of
post-Fordism have also been frequently proclaimed. In as
much as this relates to the direct organising of labour (flexibility, Toyotisation), this is, as with Taylorism, only partially
justified. A fundamental break must be noted with 'Fordism',
however, in the broader sense of parallel growth of production, productivity of labour and working-class consumption.
These postwar linkages have been pulled apart since the early
1980s; increased productivity no longer leads to more
working-class consumption.

3. *Keynesianism* is completely discredited among most economists and policymakers. Few politicians or economists still see any point in national policy, among other reasons because they say it is no longer possible in the globalised world economy – although in the wake of the Asian crisis it has become fashionable once more in restricted circles to advocate Keynesian measures. In the long run Keynes is not dead, some now say.[33] In fact, globalization alone does not explain the almost universal rejection of Keynesianism: proposals to tackle unemployment with coordinated government policies on a European scale rarely meet with a positive response, although the EU economies as a whole are large and self-sufficient enough to make European-wide Keynesianism a viable option.[34] For that matter, the US economy is also big enough and independent enough to make Keynesian policies feasible. Nonetheless, only variants of neo-classical, pro-market policy are acceptable for the reigning economic consensus.

4. *Absolute US economic hegemony* is a thing of the past, even if predictions that Europe or Japan would take over the US's economic role have turned out to be completely mistaken. Taking advantage of the dollar's central role, the growing openness of the world economy and the strength of the North American economy, from the second half of the 1980s on, the US managed increasingly to reclaim its position as the world's chief economic and military power.[35]

The steady forward-march of globalization is not *the* answer to the factors that led to the end of capitalism's postwar expansive phase. But the process of international economic restructuring, which is capital's overall response to the slowdown, is pushing globalization ahead in important ways:

- Deregulation and internationalisation have made it possible for the transport and telecommunications sectors to expand. This can shorten capital's circulation and turnover time.
- Raw materials prices continue to decline as a result of the inclusion and integration of most of the Third World in the capitalist world economy and slow economic growth rates

compared to those in the Golden Age. This makes it possible to produce more cheaply.

- Employers have managed to hold direct and indirect wage costs down by playing workers in different countries off against each other and by taking advantage of the disciplinary effects of unemployment. A sort of Gresham's Law[36] is at work on a world scale: worse working conditions are increasingly threatening better ones.[37] European chemicals companies are put under great pressure to rationalise their operations once their US competitors have managed once more to cut costs per unit of production by 5 per cent, for example; and European multinational giants like Daimler Benz, Alcatel Alsthom and Société Générale must ward off the threat of being pulled under by their US competitors by laying off tens of thousands of workers.[38]

  The mechanism is clear: it is a vicious circle. 'In a globalising economy we cannot afford any substantial wage increases, because we would then risk losing the competitive battle with countries where wages are much lower.'[39] Thanks to this mechanism the rate of exploitation has risen considerably.[40]

- No new, stable international economic or monetary order has taken shape in recent years; far from it. But there has been an uneven shift of tasks and responsibilities from national states to regional and global coordinating bodies (EU, NAFTA, G7) and towards various unelected, unaccountable institutions (World Bank, IMF, BIS, WTO, European Central Bank). For this reason, and because governments make less of an effort to direct or influence economic life, the power and influence of multinationals have increased.[41]

Was increasing globalization necessary and unavoidable? Can we draw a parallel with the determinism of the technological explanation of globalization and say that globalization was not technologically but economically determined? That would be too bold a claim; there is never only one possible way out of a crisis. We can see *now* that international economic restructuring has taken on a particular dynamic, but the development of the relationship of forces between capital and labour and within various sectors is never static. It depends on many different factors, not least on the outcome of political, socioeconomic and ideological conflicts. As explained in the last chapter, many developments and mechanisms can counteract the tendential fall in the rate of profit. Determinism can therefore be ruled out.

The Outcome So Far

The processes under way since the early 1980s have led to enormous social, cultural, economic and institutional changes. A new productive order increasingly seems to be emerging. But since everything is still in flux, it seems best to describe the current situation as a transitional one.[42] The changes have not left growth and profit rates in the industrialised countries unaffected, as we can see in Figure 4.1 and Table 4.2. But the figures show that the end of the depressive

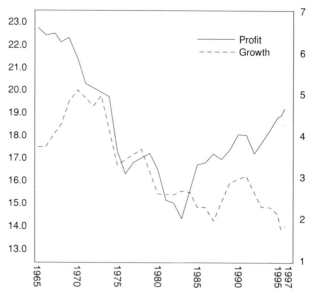

Figure 4.1 Profit and growth in seven industrialised countries (France, Germany, Italy, Japan, Spain, UK and US)[44]

long wave has still not been reached. Economic growth remains at moderate levels, well under the 4–6 per cent of the postwar period of prosperity. This has major consequences: more growth would lead to lower budget deficits (due to higher tax revenues and lower social security spending), more room for increasing real wages and decreasing social tensions as more jobs are created.

At the same time, the rate of profit has risen considerably since the early 1980s. Capitalism is developing towards a productive order in which, perhaps for the first time in history, increasing profit rates do not lead to more economic growth.[43] More profits do not lead to more jobs because investments do not go up; they are not accumulated but diverted to the financial markets. The connections between accumulation, rising productivity, economic growth and consumption that were characteristic of the postwar period of prosperity have thus broken down.

Table 4.2 Profit and growth in seven industrialised countries (France, Germany, Italy, Japan, Spain, UK and US) (%)[45]

Year	Rate of profit	Moving average rate of GNP growth
1980	15.2	3.0
1981	15.1	3.0
1982	14.3	3.0
1983	15.4	3.1
1984	16.7	3.0
1985	16.8	2.7
1986	17.2	2.7
1987	16.9	2.4
1988	17.3	2.8
1989	18.1	3.3
1990	18.1	3.3
1991	17.7	3.4
1992	18.0	3.1
1993	18.2	2.7
1994	18.7	2.7
1995	18.8	2.5
1996	19.2	2.2
1997	19.1	2.2

Since the mid-1970s the relationships between banking and industrial capital have altered on a world scale. High returns on financial assets (and speculation) have made short-term investments more attractive, while investing in the development of production has become less attractive at a time when demand is rising less rapidly thanks to stagnating wages and welfare benefits, growing inequality and decreasing public spending.[46] Higher profits do not automatically lead to expanding production: employers must expect that they can sell their products before they set about producing them. If that is not the case or if the expected returns are not high enough, then a greater proportion of profits is squirrelled away, paid out to stockholders as dividends or invested in the stock market or other financial markets. Financial revenues have increased, share ownership has been encouraged by privatisation and bank profits have risen relative to industrial profits. Multinationals' treasury departments play an active role in this ongoing financialisation, because there is much more short-term profit to be earned by trading on financial markets than by investing in new production capacity.

> The long-running bull market in the US has succeeded in creating a new group of speculators even more scary than the day traders – US corporations ... This raises the alarming prospect that the US stock market is now, to some extent, feeding on itself. Roaring share prices in internet and new technology companies – many of which are poorly understood and probably overvalued – are helping to boost the corporate profits that are fuelling this frenzied stock market.[47]

Two areas of the economy's non-financial sector must be distinguished, however. In the first area – modern industry and information services – productivity is systematically increasing, while a decreasing share of the labour force works in it. Whether companies make substantial profits or not, they persist in cutting back on personnel costs. Governments as well as companies continue to shed employees in their efforts to become 'lean and mean'. Most wage earners' buying power, and the buying power of welfare benefits even more so, is stagnating or declining, since even if these incomes rise they generally lag behind the increase in labour productivity. Income distribution is thus shifting to the detriment of wage earners, and working people's consumption is stagnating relative to production.

Who then is buying the growing mountain of products? Not governments in most countries; as a general rule they are lowering their spending. Since workers' consumption is lagging behind production, employers can only realise their profits if investment and/or consumption of the rising profits increases. But employers only invest if they have greater sales possibilities – which completes the vicious circle.

An economy that functions in this way is a low-growth economy. It is also significantly less stable than during the Fordist Golden Age, when growing production corresponded to a rising level of consumption by wage earners. A growing share of production today by contrast is destined for the global minority with substantial buying power. Because in most countries this is a small or somewhat less small minority – particularly outside the Triad – and economies of scale have become more and more important as the amounts that must be invested in new products have become greater and greater, globalization of markets, that is, operating across national frontiers, has become more crucial to producing profitably. Twenty-first-century capitalism will supposedly depend on a very heterogeneous group with buying power, 'the global middle class':

> Defining the composition of this global middle class is tricky, because of widely varying levels of development among Asian and Latin American nations ... But a reasonable estimate is that one-fourth of the world, some 1.2 billion people, enjoy middle-class lives ... [I]n the broadest sense, this new middle class can be best described as those with disposable incomes – people no longer concerned about daily survival who have joined the ranks of modern consumers.[48]

Alongside the industrial and information area there is a second area, which by its very nature is shielded from international competition and in which productivity cannot increase much or at all. This is the area where an increasing part of the labour force must somehow manage to keep a job, but where wages (and thus buying power) remain low. This area includes, for example, services such as health care, education, inexpensive housing and public transport for which there is a growing need but insufficient effective demand, because most people have little or no money to spend on them. These are services which cannot be supplied to most people at a profit – and profit is what capitalism is about. Since productivity can be raised very little in this sector and governments are not increasing spending on social and public services, this sector is growing slowly or not at all or even shrinking.

The number of badly paid, insecure, irregular jobs in personal services such as security, janitorial services, dry cleaning and catering are also definitely on the increase. Growing income inequality plays an important role here, since there is an increasing category of people who earn so much money (and have so little time) that they can easily hire ill-paid people to do the little tasks they never get to do.

Twenty-first-century capitalism thus functions in a way that implies and depends on the national and international increase in social inequality described in Chapter 1. Hardly anyone denies today that social differences have been growing since the early 1980s, though advocates of the market tend to insist that everything will turn out fine in the end.[49] There is no automatic mechanism that will make things turn out fine in the end, however. On the contrary, growing social inequality, financialisation, slow growth, price stability, dual labour markets, persistent unemployment and sharply rising profits can only be understood as parts of a coherent whole. They are all characteristic of the emerging productive order of neoliberal globalization.

A New Expansive Wave?

Since the early 1980s crucial shifts have taken place at each of the levels of the productive order that we distinguished in Chapter 3. These shifts are in part the outcome of globalization.[50]

1. *Mode of accumulation:* The relationship between banking and industrial capital has been substantially changed. Investment banking, international speculation and financial services have grown enormously.[51] In addition, while not intervening less in the economy national states are intervening in a different way (see Chapter 1). Globalization has also played a major role in shifting the relationship between capital and labour to capital's benefit (reorganisation of labour, wage structures, changing meaning of collective bargaining agreements). Finally, as we saw in the last section, a different pattern of consumption from the old, national, 'Fordist' pattern is emerging on a world scale (steady annual increase in production and, in order to sell that production, in consumption).

2. *Material forces of production:* During the current depressive long wave (by contrast with earlier historical periods) new technologies such as computers and information technology are being diffused widely without leading so far to a sharp increase in labour productivity. The economies of scale made possible by liberalisation and deregulation and the growth of the international financial sector have contributed to this phenomenon.

3. *Organisation of social relations:* At this level too globalization has major material and ideological consequences. We need only think of the way education has been subordinated to employers' requirements, changes in the social security system and further decreases of trade union influence in all sorts of advisory bodies.

4. *International division of labour:* Globalization has considerable consequences on this level too. Financial flows have not only drastically increased, but also play an important disciplinary role. Third World countries' dependency is less tied to raw materials supplies in today's world than to dependence on capital flows. The relative weight of different countries and trading blocs has shifted in major ways.

Is all this enough to launch a new expansive long wave? Apparently not. As we said before, more seems to be needed – a sharp increase in the rate of profit as well as a substantial extension of the market. This combination is crucial, but does not arise spontaneously. Nothing suggests at the moment that capital will transcend its divergent interests and priorities in order to shape an expansive productive order. For their part, the left, the trade unions and social movements have still not found adequate answers to the problems and challenges with which the neoliberal offensive and globalization confronts them.

In short, we are in a transitional situation, in a process of change whose ultimate outcome is still uncertain.[52] The future will be determined by the evolving relationship of forces between labour and capital, between industrialised countries' elites and rebellious movements in the Third World, within capital, within the workers' movement and within movements of resistance. In Chapter 5, without resorting to determinism or fatalism, we discuss a few possible outcomes.

CHAPTER 5

Globalization under Fire

Will optimism about 21st century capitalism ultimately prove misguided? Hundreds of millions of people will not benefit from this new economic order. Victims include an older generation of unemployable Russians, the uprooted of India, and the newly idle of Europe and the U.S. In its most unbridled form, capitalism certainly delivers wealth but stumbles when it comes to distributing its rewards equitably enough. Resentment against capitalism could provoke a backlash against free trade and its sponsors. And few institutions now exist to regulate the excesses of global finance and post-cold-war geopolitics.

Business Week[1]

It is a bit hard to remember what the world looked like before globalization.

Paul Krugman[2]

The collapse of bureaucratic regimes in Eastern Europe and the Soviet Union after 1989 – beginning these countries' uneven, still incomplete integration into the world market – meant the disappearance of the main bloc in the world that functioned according to a non-capitalist logic. Together with the restructuring of global capitalism since the early 1980s, this has decreased the ability of countries, particularly in the Third World, to choose any model of economic development other than neoliberalism. It also removed one of the obstacles to attacks on the gains embodied in Western European welfare states.

Anyone who has opposed globalization in the last decade or two has risked not only being excluded from the discussion, but seeming cut off from reality. You have no choice but to adapt to globalization, organisations such as the OECD have insisted, whether you like it or not. According to the reigning economic orthodoxy, unhindered movement of capital, goods and services across national frontiers leads to an optimal and thus efficient allocation of scarce resources. True, as every first-year economics student learns, efficiency and fairness are not the same thing. But as in the decades after the First World War, when the world economy was also substantially integrated, the current acceleration of economic globalization has been solidly based on an international regime of free trade in combination with free movement of capital.

Since 1997, however, both these foundation stones of increasing international economic integration have once more been put in question. We have seen that the tendency towards growing internationalisation of the world economy is real and forceful, but that the process of globalization is uneven, contradictory and certainly not linear. We have also seen that, despite the trends towards increasing globalization, no fully integrated world economy has come into existence. The world is considerably more globalised than 50 years ago, but considerably less than is theoretically conceivable.

In the coming years conflicts and contradictions will remain at work among countries, within countries, inside and among trading blocs and governments and with, among and inside institutions such as the IMF, the EU, NAFTA, the World Bank, the G7, the WTO and the BIS. Moreover, social movements and NGOs are increasingly globalising *their* networks and activities in order to wage a worldwide fight against the social and ecological effects of free trade and against the dictatorship of the financial markets. The outcome of all these processes and clashes depends on many different developments and factors. In this chapter we examine what developments may be expected in the coming years.

Back to the Future?

For the time being, the tendency towards further globalization seems likely to continue. There are many contradictions and problems; neoliberalism's credibility has suffered from the series of crises since mid-1997; there is resistance in many countries to the consequences of the reigning international economic logic; but up until now that has not had major consequences for the overall direction in which the world economy is heading.

We are living in a new era, with an international economy that is being transformed into a true world economy. The Fordist organisation of production, aimed at realising economies of scale, is being replaced in a growing number of companies and sectors with more flexible 'just-in-time' production, in which 'economies of scope' become more important.[3] Examining the drastic changes in thinking about the role of the state in the economic process may give the clearest indication that a new period has arrived. Keynes has been buried and traded in for neoliberal neoclassicists (monetarists, supply-siders, rational-expectations adepts) who assume that it is best to leave as many decisions as possible to the market.[4] Although from time to time a plea is made for a new Bretton Woods-type international monetary order – in late 1998, for example, by the then German finance minister, Oskar Lafontaine, since resigned – few people seriously think that anything will come of it in the foreseeable future.

Is a return to the Golden Age possible? To ask this question is really to ask whether the economic, social, political and institutional constellation that led to the postwar period of prosperity – the postwar productive order – can come together again. In other words, to ask the question is to answer it: as we saw in Chapter 3, the postwar expansive phase was the result of specific factors that will not recur in that particular combination.[5] It is therefore extremely improbable that we are now headed back towards the Golden Age of postwar expansion. That period was exceptional in the history of capitalism, and even if the rate of profit recovered further it would not mean a return to the postwar order. Too much has changed in the organisation and functioning of the world economy. As Joseph Schumpeter apparently once remarked: just as you can't restore the health of someone who's been run over by a truck by having the truck run him over in reverse, you can't restore an economy to health by reversing poor economic policies.[6]

To the extent that we *are* headed back to an earlier period, for much of the world population this means a return to the social relations of pre-Second World War capitalism or even longer ago. The effects of globalization sketched in Chapter 1 mean that for many people in the world *progress* is in fact *regression*. For a growing group of people in the OECD countries, postwar certainties like the right to a job, steadily increasing income, a good social system and decent public services no longer exist. For parts of the Third World as well, contrary to what is often thought and claimed, the postwar period until the early 1980s was more a time of progress (albeit minimal) than today.[7] Real wages in Mexico, for example, were on average a full 10 per cent lower at the beginning of 1995 – that is, *before* the announcement in January of President Ernesto Zedillo's plans to save the peso, which would lead to still lower wages – than they were in 1980 – even though the IMF and the World Bank pointed to Mexico for years as an example for the rest of the Third World.

Advancing globalization will make its negative effects sharper and harder. That is, there will be a greater and more dominant dictatorship of the markets, particularly over countries that wish to attract capital; greater social inequality as a result of a dual process of polarisation, within countries and on a world scale among countries; progressive levelling down of wages, working conditions and social security; ecological destruction and deterioration; a greater role for unaccountable international institutions and blocs; and a further undermining of democracy.

What will it all lead to? Not automatically to a new expansive phase, as we have seen; for that a major expansion of the market is necessary along with a considerable increase in the rate of surplus value. In the meantime, attacks on existing rights and gains continue.[8] Some observers describe these attacks as a return to the elite tactics of the early nineteenth century, when the standard responses to popular discontent were indifference and repression – tactics that at least so far have proved quite successful almost two centuries later.[9]

The counter-offensive is leading among other things to dismantling of the welfare state. But this is proceeding more slowly and with greater difficulty than many economists and politicians would like. The denial of existing rights and gains is happening bit by bit, mostly only a few small steps at a time. There has been considerable resistance.

In the Third World the economic orthodoxy of international organisations like the IMF and the World Bank has been leading for years to a form of social Darwinism.[10] This barbarism is a daily reality for many people there. Even in the improbable event that all the IMF and World Bank's pro-market prescriptions are fully carried out, this will scarcely change. World Bank economists calculated in the early 1990s that in the best case the ratio between the world's richest 20 per cent and poorest 20 per cent would have declined by 2010 from 60:1 to 50:1. But if anything at all goes wrong, they wrote, the ratio can increase further, to 70:1.[11] Since then large parts of the world have been hit by financial crises and thrown back decades in economic development. It can hardly be doubted that the more pessimistic scenario is the right one.

The First Crises of the Twenty-First Century

In the near future nothing seems able to stop the trend towards further globalization, with all the risks it entails. As we have seen in the late 1990s, the danger of a major international crisis is far from imaginary. The central problem is that little or no international regulation or control has been put in place to replace the national regulatory and control mechanisms eliminated by deregulation, privatisation and, particularly, financial innovations. Problems requiring international action are myriad, and the responsibilities and authority of organisations like the OECD, the World Bank, the IMF, the WTO, the G7, the EU and the UN are being continually reshuffled. But in the foreseeable future none of these organisations will have the resources, facilities, room and authority to impose international regulations and controls.

In addition, the dominant paradigm is still that the market should in principle solve all problems and that the risks are not as great as all that. Many facts and incidents indicate the contrary: the October 1987 stock market crash; the European Monetary System crises; the dollar crises of 1977–79 and

1986–87; the Barings Bank scandals in Singapore and England; the various Japanese banking scandals; and the collapse of the Long-Term Capital Management hedge fund in 1998.[12] Instability has increased enormously in the financial sector in particular. Compared with the 1960s, when the Bretton Woods system kept exchange rates within narrow margins and capital flows were regulated, the volatility of the financial markets has grown and grown. 'Financial crises seem now to happen with almost monotonous regularity': in addition to those just listed, 'the bond market crashed in 1994; the Mexican crisis occurred late in the same year; East Asia went into turmoil in 1997; and Russia's default and associated shock waves shook the world' in 1998.[13] No one really knows any more everything that is going on in the financial markets, what risks are being run and how great the odds are that a local crisis or stock market crash will spread, like an oil spill around the world.

The financial crises that broke out in Mexico in late 1994 and Asia in 1997 were the first major blows to the optimistic visions of progress held by globalization fans, and give a sense of the potential effects of future crises. In the Asian crisis in particular, economies that were considered powerhouses were thrown into a deep crisis from one day to the next because feelings among traders on financial markets turned against them. Millions of people suddenly lost their jobs, incomes and basic means of survival. All of the societies devastated by this crisis have experienced substantial 'erosion of their social fabric, with social unrest, more crime, more violence in the home'.[14] Now there are enthusiastic reports that growth rates and stock exchanges in these former Asian tigers are on the upswing. But it will be many years before the sharply increased unemployment and poverty can be brought back even to pre-crisis levels.

The Asian crisis is to students of financial markets what 'the collapse of the Eastern Bloc was to Sovietologists'.[15] Thanks to it, the position that financial markets are always efficient cannot be taken seriously. Traders' sheep-like behaviour and short-term thinking led in Asia and Latin America to 'self-fulfilling crises' and overblown exchange rate fluctuations. Despite all the lovely stories and conferences about the necessity of reforming the 'international financial architecture', nothing has changed. Everyone is just waiting for the next financial crisis.

Hardly anyone dared predict that neoliberal globalization would lead to such turmoil before the Mexican crisis – widely seen as the first crisis of the new globalised world – actually broke out in 1994. Mexico was the Rolls Royce among 'emerging markets'. In 1994 it was the first Third World country to be admitted to the OECD. That same year it joined the US and Canada to form the free-trade zone NAFTA. It was *the* example of successful neoliberal structural adjustment policies that the IMF and the World Bank preached to the South and East. But on 20 December 1994 the fairy tale was suddenly over. The peso lost over 40 per cent of its value, the stock market collapsed, and the government failed completely to stop capital flight, despite a tough austerity package. The crisis had arrived, and for the time being no end seemed in sight.

Politics and economics are always closely linked; but the Mexican power structure's reproach that the Zapatista uprising in Chiapas against NAFTA and single-party rule had caused the peso crisis was far too flattering. The Zapatistas' occupation of a few villages simply confirmed once more what the world already knew, that social inequality in Mexico is immense and that there are people there who refuse to accept it.[16] Perhaps this was shocking news for some investors and speculators. But the crisis's fundamental cause was something else: the fact that, from a strictly economic standpoint, the neoliberal project simply cannot work.

With far-reaching deregulation, privatisation and market liberalisation, Mexico has opened its doors wide to foreign capital. Everything is aimed at exports. But there are many other countries who also want to increase their share of export markets. Furthermore, inside NAFTA Mexico, as a Third World country, is in no way comparable to the world's premiere capitalist country, the US. As Mexican exports increased, its imports increased much more. The resulting balance of payments deficit rose to $28 billion, over 7 per cent of Mexico's GNP. The deficit was covered by capital imports; but much of the capital flowing into Latin Amerca was speculative or was used to buy companies that were being sold cheap as part of privatisation schemes. This was an extremely volatile, uncertain and unstable inward flow. The slightest upset turned the inward flow into an outward flow.

To save what was still savable President Zedillo announced a harsh austerity package. This was a rude awakening, particularly for those who had voted for him a few months before. Zedillo's campaign promises had been 4 per cent growth, many new jobs and 'prosperity for your family'. One of his slogans was: 'He knows how to do it.' Indeed, he did. The emergency package led to a recession, with higher interest rates, lower investment and consumption, problem-plagued banks and companies, sharply higher inflation and rapidly rising unemployment. A Brazilian weekly remarked shrewdly soon after the crisis broke out: 'The real Mexico was a poor country that acted like a rich country. The party is over for the Mexican middle class. The party for the working class, that hadn't even begun, has been postponed indefinitely.'[17]

In the wake of the Mexican crisis the stock market fell in Argentinia, Brazil and Chile, and the exchange rates of many currencies such as the Brazilian real came under pressure. In Latin America they called this the 'tequilla effect', but the crisis had effects elsewhere as well. Government bond prices fell in Nigeria, Bulgaria, Morocco and Russia, while the US dollar also declined. This Mexican crisis 'radiation' highlighted for the first time an explosive problem in the current world economy: thanks to the international regulatory vacuum, a crisis in one country can spread rapidly, and even lead to a worldwide financial crisis in which one stock market after another and one exchange rate after another threaten to fall like dominos. In 1997 and 1998 the same phenomenon was visible once more on an even greater scale.

While the reigning economic orthodoxy was and is that as much as possible must be left to the market, the time had come to lend the invisible hand a helping hand – since major financial institutions threatened to go under. On 31 January 1995 President Bill Clinton presented an international aid programme to contain the Mexican crisis – just in time, since the Mexican central bank had virtually exhausted its reserves and the moment was rapidly approaching when Mexico would have had to announce a moratorium on debt payments. That, according to IMF director Michel Camdessus, would have led to a true global catastrophe. The alarm was sounded, with even a touch of panic. Clinton was not managing to round up enough support in the US Senate for the rescue package he had announced immediately after the outbreak of the crisis.

At the World Economic Forum in Davos, where the world's top managers, central bankers and finance ministers gather each year, a discussion was organised on the question of where the next crisis would explode: Hungary, China, Argentina, Indonesia? Guru George Soros among others gave the opinion that a catastrophe was looming: a new stock market crash as in 1987, not just in Mexico but on Wall Street and in London, Frankfurt, Tokyo and Hong Kong. 'Plan B' was hastily started up. Clinton did an end run around the Senate by using special presidential powers. The IMF and the BIS came forward with the largest amounts they had ever spent. All told, the Mexican government temporarily had over $50 billion to spend. Not that this was much of a gift: the money would have to be paid back, and would only be available when major cuts dictated by the IMF had been carried out. Mexico also had to pledge its oil revenues as security, and interest had to be paid on the loans. By the end of 1995 Mexico's foreign debt reached over $170 billion. In 1995 alone $57 billion in interest and principal payments were made: more than the total paid to foreign creditors from 1821 to 1976.

The package put together by Clinton was called many different things: 'a disaster plan', 'the last resort', 'the emergency brake', and even, harking back to the Gulf War, 'financial operation Desert Storm'.[18] But the interesting question is: what were the world's richest countries really so anxious about? Why did they, together with the IMF and the BIS, put together the biggest aid package in history for a country like Mexico?

There were several reasons. First and foremost, they were afraid that the crisis would spread uncontrollably if Mexico stopped making payments. The 'system risk' so feared by economists and bankers genuinely existed, thanks to the greatly increased integration of financial markets.

Second, the Mexican economy could not be allowed to collapse completely because it was the showcase example of the 'emerging markets'. Mexico was cited up until the day the peso crisis broke out as proof that IMF policies are the way to prosperity and happiness. Averting its collapse was seen as crucial to saving the IMF's credibility.

A third reason for the aid package had to do with the US position in the world. NAFTA could not be allowed to fail, because the free trade treaty's success and future enlargement is a major part of the US strategy to improve its position in the world economy. NAFTA's collapse would be very disadvantageous for the US's global economic role.

There was, finally, a fourth reason. Vast interests were at stake; if Mexico had had to announce a moratorium on its debt payments, investment funds, banks and speculators would have lost large sums of money. The aid package was in fact a gift from the taxpayers to the rich.[19] One of the rich people in question was US Treasury Secretary Robert Rubin, who played a key role in arranging the aid programme. Before Rubin became secretary of the treasury he was vice-chairman of the board of Goldman Sachs, one of the US's largest brokerage houses. In 1992, Rubin's last year there, Goldman Sachs made a profit of $1.4 billion from, among other things investments in Mexico. The brokerage house was one of the largest donors to Clinton's presidential campaign, and Secretary Rubin had an estimated net worth of more than $150 million in 1995.

In the light of this background to the international aid programme, it is hardly surprising that all the anxiety over the state of the world economy did not include much concern for the effects on ordinary Mexicans. These effects have been immense. As a result of sharply higher interest rates, cuts in government spending and declining buying power Mexico went into a deep recession. More than a million Mexicans lost their jobs; more than half of Mexicans now live officially in poverty. Per capita income fell in 1995 from $3800 to $2600, the lowest level since 1989. No wonder that crime rates and suicide rates have risen rapidly and that many Mexicans must manage to survive by working in the informal sector.

The Mexican crisis showed how unstable and incalculable the world economy was. In its wake the G7 wrung its hands

over the lack of 'global governance'. They decided that the
IMF should work more closely with the World Bank and the
WTO in order to signal more quickly where things risk going
wrong. They also agreed to support initiatives that would give
the IMF more funds so that it could react quickly in case of
another Mexico. With the decision to give the IMF extra
resources to act quickly when fresh disasters occur, the
world's most important heads of government tacitly admitted
that neither the IMF nor any other organisation can *prevent*
new crises.

This has since been confirmed many times over by the
financial crises of 1997–98. In the months following the
Mexican crisis commentators and analysts from international
organisations warned that there would be more crises, though
nobody knew where or when. Sooner than many expected it
became clear that the next Mexicos were to be found in Asia,
where from mid-1997 on one Tiger economy after another
fell into a deep crisis. The crisis and its shock waves then
spread to other continents, leading to dramatic impoverish-
ment and lasting negative consequences for the growth
perspectives of the world economy as a whole. It 'prompted
some radical new thinking', with well-known economists
openly doubting central elements of the dominant orthodoxy
of free trade and free capital flows.[20]

The globalization of the Southeast Asian crisis came as a
very unwelcome shock to protagonists of free trade and financial liberalisation, who had presented the development of
these Asian economies as the ultimate proof that their policies
work better than old-style import-substitution strategies. To
cite only one typical account by a free-trade champion
(published ironically enough in 1997 under the title 'How We
Learn'):

At the same time as evidence of the high costs of import-
substitution regimes was accumulating, another important
development occurred. Starting first in Taiwan, several
East Asian economies began growing rapidly under policies
diametrically opposite to those prevalent under import
substitution ... [T]he East Asian experiences demon-
strated, as nothing else could have, the feasibility and

viability of alternative trade policies ... They also showed
that rates of growth well above those realized even in the
most rapidly growing import-substitution countries such as
Brazil and Turkey could be realized.[21]

In the light of these ideas, it is no accident that the IMF did
not foresee the crisis in Asia. Less than three months before
the crisis broke out in South Korea, it wrote: 'Directors
welcomed Korea's continued impressive macroeconomic
performance and praised the authorities for their enviable
fiscal record.' With Thailand on the verge of financial
collapse, it 'strongly praised Thailand's remarkable economic
performance and the authorities' consistent record of sound
macroeconomic policies'.[22] The same indestructible confidence in free trade and financial liberalisation policies was
expressed in the IMF negotiators' demands on countries in
need of financial support. Even a mainstream economist notes
that 'once the crisis struck, Asian countries found their
policies largely dictated by Washington – that is, by the
International Monetary Fund and the U.S. Treasury'.[23]

International organisations, economists and policymakers
also seriously underestimated the consequences of the Asian
crisis for the world economy as a whole. According to the Ten
Commandments of neoliberal globalization that had become
ever more rigid since the late 1970s, deregulation, privatisation, trade liberalisation, free capital movements, a shrinking
social and public sector and more market discipline were
supposed to ensure global prosperity and abundance. From
this point of view a crisis here or there could not end the fun
in the rest of the world. But those selling these neoliberal
prayer beads threatened to become victims of their own
success. The celebrated liberalisation, deregulation and internationalisation have created new forms of dependency, and in
times of economic adversity they provide transmission routes
along which crises spread and multiply. By 1998 one country
after another, including Russia and Brazil, were hit by
currency speculation, falling stock markets, capital flight,
declining foreign investment and lower growth projections.
The *Wall Street Journal* warned of a 'financial Vietnam', while
super-speculator George Soros spoke of a 'crisis of globalised

capitalism'.[24] Tens of millions lost their jobs in 1997–98, amidst reports of a major increase in child prostitution in many countries as they slid into poverty.

How did the IMF, backed by its shareholders, the world's rich countries, react? It made the situation still worse by posing sado-monetarist conditions for aid to countries in difficulties. An almost perfect inversion of the Keynesian compact lay at the core of the policies imposed by Washington over the last few years on one country after another: 'faced with an economic crisis, countries are urged to raise interest rates, slash spending, and increase taxes.' Apparently, no one except the all-too-eager hedge funds was responsible for these counterproductive policies. 'The rules of the New World Order, it seemed, offered developing countries no way out. And so it was really nobody's fault that things turned out so badly.'[25] The IMF makes demands that exacerbate crises, ones that are based simply on the market-based principle that countries must win back the 'confidence' of the financial markets as quickly as possible.

No one could ask for a more telling illustration of the perverse, anti-social logic of today's neoliberal globalization. In order to offer speculators and investors a sufficient perspective of profits, governments on the threshold of the twenty-first century must deepen recessions, destroy jobs on a massive scale and slash away even more at social and other spending.

It has become steadily clearer in recent decades that the strategy of export-led growth proposed and imposed by the IMF, Wall Street and the rich countries' governments is unworkable for more and more 'emerging markets'. The financial markets have become all-powerful thanks to the far-reaching globalization of the world economy, and as a result the needs of the Third World's population are sacrificed. The globalising world economy reproduces and reinforces domination by capital. Fortunately, the central building blocks of the neoliberal order – free movement of capital and free trade – are increasingly being challenged. In various countries and movements an alternative agenda is taking shape for a 'negotiated and selective integration with the world economy',[26] which means among other things: controls on capital flows; fiscal reforms based on a progressive tax system; land reform;

priority for domestic development rather than exports; economic democracy, so as to let communities, citizens' groups and popular movements decide the main priorities for economic development; and priority to sustainability, given the major environmental problems in the countries in crisis. Until programmes of this kind based on a different economic and social logic are carried out, much of the world population will remain the plaything of financial market traders and multinational managers making decisions behind their backs.

Meanwhile, fresh financial crises can reinforce nationalist, chauvinist and protectionist tendencies, which are already on the rise, and lead to their triumph. Some observers say that contradictions between increasing globalization and the decreasing functionality of the national state are insoluble, and predict that they will mount until they result in chaos.[27] Others assume that contradictions among the big economic powers will grow, and suggest ominously that new military conflicts are possible. The fact that cooperation is rational should not lead us to conclude that the powers will in fact always cooperate:

> Only a few months before the guns opened fire in 1914, Norman Angell, a famous contemporary economic pundit, had predicted in his book *The Age of Illusion* that the degree of interdependence of the major European economies had made war no longer conceivable.[28]

The outcome of a future crisis cannot be determined in advance, however; nor does it depend on any economic laws. It depends on the development of national and global struggles.[29]

Towards a Different Economic Logic

Crises, chaos or the collapse of the international financial system are not the only ways by which the apparently unstoppable trend towards globalization can come to a halt. A less apocalyptic variant is also conceivable, one in which other economic and social priorities replace the profit-driven logic of capitalism. Many elements of such a positive alternative have been assembled in recent years by social movements North and South, East and West. The failure of the Multilateral Agreement on Investment and the 1999 WTO Seattle summit have increased their confidence that such an alternative may be attainable.

Neoliberals have responded to these setbacks by insisting even more shrilly that there *is* no alternative. The real losers in the Seattle conference's failure were the more than five billion inhabitants of the developing countries, they cried.[30] But even demagogy has its limits: the US and EU negotiators who shed tears over the negative effects of the conference's failure on the world's poor were primarily interested in their own – in part clashing – interests and trading priorities. The EU, for example, wanted to put new items on the WTO agenda in order to eliminate barriers to Northern multinationals' access to Southern markets, while the EU itself still heavily subsidises its agricultural exports. Progressives in the Third World tend in any event to see the Seattle conference's failure as a gain for developing countries, not a loss.[31]

Can anything be done not just to slow down, but actually to counter the headlong rush towards globalization? Many proposals have been made in recent years to make the world somewhat less unjust and limit somewhat the power of financial markets and speculators, such as: cancellation (or reduction) of Third World countries' debts; an international tax on air travel, levied at each airport, to fund international development aid; an EU social charter guaranteeing basic rights such as health care, education, jobs and decent incomes for all Europeans; the 'Tobin tax' of say 0.5 per cent proposed by Nobel Prize winner James Tobin on all currency transactions;[32] controls and limits on capital flows; more regulation of derivatives trading; and so forth.

Is there any hope for such proposals in the globalised world economy? Some observers say that, while these proposals focus attention on the nature of the problem, '[p]ractical recommendations must acknowledge the powerful forces promoting the growth of capital flows'.[33] But it is also practical to envisage the outright defeat of these 'powerful forces'. We have already seen that, while the functions of states have changed, states are definitely still playing a role and there are still choices to make about how they play it. Opponents of more regulation and active state intervention admit this. Even *The Economist* has rejected the idea that states are now powerless. Politicians are all too eager to use the drastic changes in the world to justify their abandonment of old political objectives and ideals. In reality, while it is not easy to rebuild fire walls that politicians have spent decades knocking down, it is far from impossible.[34]

A striking side-effect of the Seattle fiasco is that assertions treated for years as knock-down, discussion-closing arguments are suddenly phrased in a more nuanced way. People now recall, for example, that 'the first global economy' fell apart with the arrival of the First World War, even though everyone thought then as now that global economic integration was unstoppable.[35] The progress of globalization no longer seems guaranteed. It seems possible after all that the strong technological forces propelling the world towards further economic integration 'can be slowed, if not halted'.[36]

Even the business press is making a bit of room now and then for a dissident who says that the forces of globalization not only can be stopped, but should be stopped. One columnist profaned the pages of *Business Week* with the headline, 'The Seattle Protesters Got It Right', explaining: 'The WTO agenda is set by the world's leading governments, which forgot that they are elected not only to advance the interests of multinational corporations but also those of citizens.'[37] One self-declared mainstream Harvard economist spoke up, not for the first time, against treating the means – trade – as if it were an end in itself. Instead of asking what kind of trading system is best for trade, he said, we should ask which is best to help people to uphold their values and reach their development objectives.[38] These are not the kind of comments the WTO likes to hear. They imply, for example, that poor countries should have the right to prioritise fighting poverty instead of increasing exports.

It is clearly possible to throw a certain amount of sand in the machinery of globalization and market orthodoxy, if only the political will for it exists. However important such small changes and improvements can be – and they are in themselves very worthy of support – only symptoms are being combated and not the disease as long as the fundamental characteristics and laws of motion of the world capitalist system remain unaffected. Social inequality, ecological destruction, oppression and exploitation of the Third World, the further undermining of democracy and the levelling down of wages, working conditions and social security will continue to increase as long as the existing economic logic is not radically overhauled. The possibility of international crises, with possible regression towards nationalism, protectionism and chauvinism as a result, will also continue to exist.

It is not possible within the existing economic logic, in which profit maximisation comes first, to solve the most important problems that humanity faces. Under capitalism, the individual interests of speculators, employers or investors determine what they do. The partial rationality of their actions clashes with the general social interest of present and future generations.

In fact, capitalism is becoming more and more irrational. The discrepancy between what is economically and socially possible and what is actually happening has never been greater than it is today. Criticisms of free-trade ideology are exposing year by year more and more of the system's flaws. For several years, for example, the environmental movement has been pointing out the ecological costs of unrestricted trade in the interest of profit maximisation. How 'free' are poor countries with enormous burdens of debt who earn money on the world's toxic waste market by allowing the dumping of poison from the rich West? The WTO, the IMF and the rich Western countries preach trade liberalisation as a universally valid prescription; but movements in the North and the South are resisting the attack this implies for countries' democratic right, particularly in the Third World, to choose a development path in the interests of their own peoples.

The world could look very different if priorities were determined in a truly democratic way, instead of according to the principle of 'one dollar, one vote'. More and more people are arriving at the conclusion that revolutionary changes are both necessary and objectively possible.

Action by living, breathing social forces can transform even the most seemingly inextricable economic and political situation. More than ever before, an alternative must take into account a number of different dimensions:

- The political dimension. Although governments have deliberately cast aside a part of their regulatory functions to allow for the deregulation of capital flows, they can be pressured into reinstating these functions. It is a question of political will; if those in power cannot rise to the task, they can either step aside or be ousted.
- The dimensions of citizenship and class. Those 'from below' and their organisations – whether from the labour movement born in the nineteenth century (parties, unions), from other grassroots movements or from new social movements born in the latter half of the twentieth century – must reclaim their right to intervene in society and exercise control over certain aspects of public life, to exert pressure on other political and economic players and to raise in concrete terms the question of hands-on political power.
- The economic dimension. Economic decisions lie at the core of all the other dimensions. Such decisions should be directed at placing restrictions on capital flows and on those that control them, the holders of capital. The recent evolution of capitalism has given renewed urgency to the debate on new forms of radicalism.[39]

What would an alternative look like? As we have seen, many different ideas exist, but there are two core questions that must be answered in order to arrive at a different economic and social logic.[40] First, how and by what social forces should the priorities and direction of economic development be decided? Today this is done behind everyone's back by the 'invisible hand' of the market and in multinationals' boardrooms. Second, what kind of relationship and engagement with the world market is wanted? This means that financial deregulation and fair trade must be put on the agenda. Developing an alternative means discussing the economic, social, political and institutional conditions under which the current downwards spiral – progress equals regression – can be reversed. This can happen only on the basis of a radically different starting point: that production should be organised not so as to make the highest possible profits, but to meet the needs of the whole world population.

The essence of what is necessary can really be summed up in one phrase: drastic redistribution and democratisation of resources and structures. Many more collective debates, analyses, experiments and experiences, by workers, young people, women, activists and scholars in and with social movements, are needed to determine exactly what this means concretely. Their topics will undoubtedly include the following issues.

Reregulation of the financial sector

Bringing the financial sector under social control so as to put an end to speculation and economic sabotage, so that democratic decisions can be reached regarding how much resources should be devoted to what ends. Naturally, all small steps in this direction, such as the introduction of a Tobin tax on financial transactions, are worthy of support.

Cancellation of Third World debt

A radical break with exploitation of the Third World, to be replaced with cooperation on the basis of mutual interest. This means the payment of fair prices for Third World products and the cancellation of Third World debt, which has already been repaid many times over.[41]

Break with export-led growth

A break with the export-led growth propagated and imposed all over the world by the IMF, the World Bank, the WTO and the OECD, so as to give priority to domestic development and the organising of production to meet local and regional needs.

Sustainable production

A transition from the current wasteful and polluting ways of production to ecologically responsible, sustainable production. This requires a planned (how else could it be done?) global redivision of the world's environmental carrying capacity – that is, first, a prudent estimate of the maximum allowable annual usage of finite resources (like oil) and the maximum allowable annual level of activities (like car production) that would otherwise endanger the preservation of the biosphere; and, second, a democratically decided, equitable allocation of these annual maximums among the world's population.[42] By contrast with the current situation, economic growth will not be an end in itself within such an alternative logic, but will be subordinated to the planned satisfaction of the needs of the world's total current and future population.

Control over the labour process

A fundamental change in the current, management-dominated labour processes by introducing structures and processes controlled and initiated by all working people. Also giving a high priority to everyone's personal development and work satisfaction so as to make optimal use of the now largely unused creativity, knowledge and insights of the people who do the work every day.[43] Consumers and producers of goods and services can also ensure a far more sustainable satisfaction of needs.

Redistribution of work

Drastic redistribution of paid work by introducing shorter working hours with no cut in pay, so that everyone can benefit from rising productivity instead of only a small minority as is now the case, and so that everyone who can and wants to work can have a job. Drastic redistribution of unpaid work as well through socialisation of household tasks and through a shorter work week that gives everyone more time for caretaking tasks.

Redistribution of income

Drastic redistribution of income and wealth from the small group of the most highly paid and rich people to those without assets and the lower-paid, and establishment of a maximum income alongside a global minimum income for everyone. Good, free, basic public services – education, health care, public transport, housing and culture – belong in this same framework.

Democracy and planning

A break with the reigning orthodoxy of more and more market. Mechanisms and structures should be established for democratic discussion, decision-making and planning – that is, jointly by *everyone* – of the chief directions and priorities for economic development, in a socially and ecologically responsible way.[44]

Changes like these will require considerable social pressure, unrest, and the building of stronger organisations and movements. Without any doubt, there will be conflicts with the dominant elites that benefit from the status quo. Rebuilding the left, the trade union movement and other social movements is essential if these battles are to be won.

A new reinforcement of organisations and movements for social change requires more than recalling and defending past experiences. The world has changed in fundamental ways, and this will have consequences for the structure, themes and methods of work of opposition movements. The most important change that virtually all leftist organisations and social movements will have to make is a shift to functioning outside their old, almost exclusively national frameworks. In making this shift, they can take advantage of the great potential of new technologies like the Internet.

Paradoxically, the right and employers are far better organised internationally than the left and the unions, whose language is traditionally much more internationalist. In other social movements cross-border organising is already more common. All over the world activists in environmental, soli-

darity, youth, immigrant, women's and lesbian/gay organisations are hard at work on globalization from below. There is
also never an IMF, World Bank, OECD, EU or G8 summit
without NGOs organising a parallel counter-summit and all
sorts of street actions. But when most organisations in the
workers' movement draw up their budgets and work plans,
international cooperation and solidarity are still an after-
thought. As long as many unions and left-wing parties are
protective of 'national' interests, furthermore, the right and
employers can easily play working and poor people in
different countries off against each other. As long as this does
not change there will be little social change, and even
powerful organisations like the union movement are doomed
to become more and more marginal.

That would be very serious. An effective response to the
current neoliberal globalization must in the first place be
economic, and thus must rely on the world's working and
poor people. Interestingly, possibilities and points of depar-
ture for internationalising trade union work are multiplying
with each new forward surge of globalization. Since companies are organising parts of their production, administration,
assembly and sales internationally, and international
takeovers, mergers and joint ventures are on the increase, new
relations and contacts are being made between employees in
different countries who all work for the same firm or are part
of the same chain of production. Changes in the organisation
of labour (such as 'just-in-time' production with the smallest
possible inventories) also make production processes vulner-
able in new ways to worker action. If a strike breaks out
anywhere in the chain of production, within a few days other
links will be paralysed by parts shortages.

This increases the possibilities of connections and common
interests in international trade union work. A fine example of
where this can lead: when Ford factory workers in Cuatitlan,
north of Mexico City, struck in 1994 against layoffs and for
better working conditions, members of United Auto Workers
in a US Ford factory sent money to support the action. Their
reasoning was: if the Mexicans win, that's good for us as well
as them because Ford won't be so quick to (threaten to) move
production to Mexico.[45] There are many other such possibil-

ities for intensive contacts and common actions by unions in different countries. The time is more than ripe for coordinating demands and actions in different parts of international concerns like Renault, Unilever and Shell. It is high time for at least a European trade union and welfare-recipient offensive in order to fight for a much shorter working week with no cut in pay and an expanded public sector.

It is also necessary and possible to go beyond internationalising trade union work in single companies. Employers are playing workers off against each other everywhere and taking advantage of worsening working conditions at competing companies in order to lower their own companies' norms. This increases the objective possibilities of international trade union strategies for entire industries at a European or international level. Most industries are dominated by two or three companies; if wage earners in those few firms succeed in preventing workers in one company from being played off against workers in another, the race to the bottom in wages, benefits and working conditions can be slowed down or reversed. This would indeed require a radical change of course by most trade unions. Other social movements and leftist parties face the same task. In some countries we are beginning to see that more militant unions are developing into broader social movements. This may well become one of the most effective new responses to globalization.[46]

On the threshold of the twenty-first century the left, the trade union movement and other social movements face a fundamental challenge. In the face of cynicism, fatalism and the dominant market orthodoxy, a social, ecological, feminist and internationalist alternative must win back credibility and offer new hope by developing realistic utopias. We must show in practice that and how a different logic is possible. New experiences and initiatives, new forms of practical internationalism based on solidarity and educated self-interest, will be decisive to turning the tide.

Notes

Introduction

1. *Business Week*, 3 Oct. 1994.
2. Doug Henwood, 'A daily report from the World Trade Organization summit, Seattle', 4 Dec. 1999, distributed on Left Business Observer email list.
3. Paul Krugman, 'Reckonings: once and again', *New York Times*, 2 Jan. 2000.
4. *Financial Times*, 11 Oct. 1999.
5. 'The anxiety behind globalization', *Business Week*, 20 Dec. 1999.
6. *Business Week*, 27 Dec. 1999.
7. See, for example, the *Financial Times*, 28 Dec. 1999.
8. For analyses and facts about these institutions, see Eric Toussaint and Peter Drucker eds, *IMF/World Bank/WTO: The Free-Market Fiasco*, Amsterdam: IIRE, 1995, and Eric Toussaint, *Your Money or Your Life!: The Tyranny of Global Finance*, London: Pluto Press, 1998.
9. Ricardo Petrella, 'Les nouvelles Tables de la Loi', *Le Monde Diplomatique*, Oct. 1995.
10. Bank for International Settlements, *64th Annual Report*, Basle: BIS, 1994, p. 211.
11. Richard Barnet & John Cavanagh, *Global Dreams: Imperial Corporations and the New World Order*, New York: Simon & Schuster, 1994, p. 423; *Financial Times* (30 Aug. 1994).
12. Ludo Cuyvers, 'Naar nieuwe internationale spelregels?', *Maandschrift Economie* no. 58 (1994), p. 245.
13. 'It is perhaps not surprising that progress has been slowest in the area of international transactions. It is there that competitive forces are strongest and voluntary cooperation indispensable. It is there, too, that the tension between the borderless nature of finance and essentially national, not necessarily consistent legal frameworks is most apparent.' (BIS, *64th Annual Report*, p. 190)

Chapter 1

1. Manfred Bienefeld, 'Capitalism and the nation state in the dog days of the twentieth century', in Ralph Miliband and Leo Panitch eds, *Socialist Register 1994: Between Globalism and Nationalism*, London: Merlin Press, 1994, p. 94.
2. Jos Teunissen & Cees Veltman, 'De angst voor de norm', *Hervormd Nederland*, 26 Aug. 1995, p. 12.
3. Jacobus Andriessen & Rob van Esch, 'Globalisering: een zekere trend', *Discussienota* vol. 3 no. 1, The Hague: Ministerie van Economische Zaken, 1993; K. Ohmae, *The End of the Nation State*, New York: Free Press, 1995; Robert Reich, *The Work of Nations*, New York: Vintage Books, 1992.
4. Ellen Meiksins Wood, '"Globalization" or "globaloney"', *Monthly Review* (Feb. 1997), pp. 21–32.
5. Winfried Ruigrok & Rob van Tulder, *The Logic of International Restructuring*, London: Routledge, 1995; Ruigrok & van Tulder, 'Misverstand globalisering', *Economisch Statistische Berichten*, 25 Dec. 1995, pp. 1140–43; Alfred Kleinknecht & Jan ter Wengel, 'Feiten over globalisering', *Economisch Statische Breichten* (6 Oct. 1996), pp. 831–33; Meiksins Wood, '"Globalization" or "globaloney"'; David Gordon, 'The global economy: New edifice or crumbling foundations?', *New Left Review* no. 168 (Mar.–Apr. 1988), pp. 24–64.
6. Robert Boyer & Daniel Drache, *States against Markets*, London: Routledge, 1996; Paul Hirst & Graham Thompson, *Globalization in Question*, Cambridge: Polity Press, 1996; Elmar Altvater & Birgit Mahnkopf, *Grenzen der Globalisierung*, Münster: Westfälisches Dampfboot, 1996. One example is the simplistic claim that in today's globalised world national states no longer make a difference to technological development. Various contributions to a book edited by Archibugi and Michie show, however, that 'the thesis that might be dubbed "techno-nationalism" is not necessarily contradicted by what might at first sight appear to be the alternative thesis, "techno-globalism". The two concepts describe, rather, two strictly interrelated aspects of contemporary technological change. Certainly, a globalised economy is transforming the landscape for the generation and diffusion of innovation, but this does not appear to decrease the importance of national characteristics or, even less, of national institutions and their policies. On the contrary, by magnifying the potential costs and benefits that will result from any one country's competitive advantage or disadvantage – as a growing proportion of the home markets risks being lost to imports, while a growing proportion of domestic output may be dependent on winning export

orders – globalization will increase the impact which national policy will have on domestic living standards.' (Daniele Archibugi & Jonathan Michie, 'Technological globalisation and national systems of innovation: An introduction', in Archubugi & Michie eds, *Technology, Globalisation and Economic Performance,* Cambridge: Cambridge University Press, 1997)

7.   Gérard Kébabdjian, *L'économie mondiale: Enjeux nouveaux, nouvelles théories,* Paris: Editions du Seuil, 1994, pp. 26–27.

8.   See A. Glyn & B. Sutcliffe, 'Global but leaderless?: The new capitalist order', in Ralph Miliband & Leo Panitch eds, *Socialist Register 1992: New World Order?,* London: Merlin Press, 1992, p. 77; Mensink & van Bergeijk, 'Globlablablah', p. 915.

9.   Charles Oman, 'Technological change, globalisation of production and the role of multinationals', *Innovations: Cahiers d'économie de l'innovation* vol. 5 (1997), p. 15.

10. François Chesnais, 'Mondialisation du capital et régime d'accumulation à dominante financière', *Agones: Philosophie, Critique & Littérature* vol. 16 (1996), p. 27. See also Wladimir Andreff, *Les multinationales globales,* Paris: La Découverte, 1996.

11. John Grieve Smith, 'Devising a strategy for pay', in Michie & Grieve Smith, *Employment and Economic Performance: Jobs, Inflation and Growth,* Oxford: Oxford University Press, 1997, p. 206.

12. For analyses and criticism of these policies, see Michel Husson, *Misère du capital: Une critique du néoliberalisme,* Paris: Syros, 1996; Hoang Ngoc Liêm, *Salaires et emploi: Une critique de la pensée unique,* Paris: Syros, 1996; Pedro Montes, *El desorden neoliberal,* Madrid: Editorial Trotta, 1996; Eric Toussaint & Peter Drucker eds, *IMF/World Bank/WTO: The Free-Market Fiasco,* Amsterdam: IIRE, 1995.

13. As early as 1848 Marx and Engels wrote in the *Communist Manifesto* about industrial products that were consumed throughout the world and the universal interdependence of countries on one another (cited in Michie & Grieve Smith, 1995, p. xv). And in 1969 *Fortune* magazine said that companies everywhere were operating across national boundaries, causing tensions between the way the world was organised politically and the way it was to a growing extent organised economically (*Fortune,* 15 Aug. 1969, cited in Robin Murray, 'The internationalization of capital and the nation state', *New Left Review* no. 67 (1971), p. 85).

14. Source: M. Kitson & Jonathan Michie, 'Trade and growth: A historical perspective', in Michie & John Grieve Smith eds,

Managing the Global Economy, Oxford: Oxford University Press, 1995, p. 8.

15. Ruigrok & van Tulder, 'Misverstand globalisering', p. 1141.

16. Kleinknecht & Ter Wengel, 'Feiten over globalisering', use the same table in their article, but they write that research by economic historians shows that the figure for the Netherlands in 1913 was not 100 but 70, because much trade in those days was purely for transit. The arithmetical average for 1913 in that case becomes 37.6, which would totally disprove Ruigrok's and Van Tulder's claim that the world economy today is hardly more open than in 1913. As an aside, it is somewhat bizarre to work with arithmetical rather than weighted averages.

17. Douglas Irwin ('The United States in a new global economy?: A century's perspective', *American Economic Review* vol. 86 no. 2 (1996), pp. 41–46) and concludes that the export of tradeables from the US has increased more than Ruigrok and Van Tulder's statistics would indicate. Along the same lines, Kees van Paridon ('Een relevantere handelsmaatstaf', *Economisch Statistische Berichten* [6 Nov. 1996]) calculates that conclusions other than Ruigrok and Van Tulder's can be drawn if the trade flows are corrected for products that are not tradeable or hardly so. Nico Mensink and Peter van Bergeijk, who work at the Dutch Department of Economic Affairs, criticise the data used by Ruigrok and Van Tulder ('Globlablablah', *Economisch Statistische Berichten* [6 Nov. 1996]).

18. P. Bowles & B. MacLean, 'Regional blocs: Can Japan be the leader?', in Boyer & Drache, *States against Markets.*

19. Dani Rodrik, *The New Global Economy and Developing Countries: Making Openness Work,* Washington: Johns Hopkins University Press, 1999, p. 9.

20. BIS, *64th Annual Report,* Basel: BIS, 1994.

21. Birgit Slot & Laurens Meijaard, 'Het dictaat van de kapitaalstromen', *Economisch Statistiche Berichten,* 31 Aug. 1994, p. 784.

22. UNCTAD, *World Investment Report 1998: Trends and Determinants,* New York: UNCTAD, 1998.

23. J. Eatwell, 'The international origins of unemployment', in Michie & Grieve Smith, *Employment and Economic Performance,* p. 277.

24. BIS press release, 10 May 1999.

25. Source: Olivier Piot, *Finance et économie: La fracture,* Paris: Le Monde-Editions, 1995, pp. 38–39.

26. Richard Barnet & John Cavanagh, *Global Dreams: Imperial Corporations and the New World Order,* New York: Simon & Schuster, 1994, p. 17.

27. *Economist*, 7 Oct. 1995, pp. 12, 34; Andrew Walter, *World Power and World Money*, New York: Harvester Wheatsheaf, 1993, p. 199.

28. François Chesnais, *Tobin or not Tobin?: Une taxe internationale sur le capital*, Paris: L'Esprit Frappeur, 1999, p. 10.

29. Alan Greenspan, speech in Boca Ratan, Florida, 19 Mar. 1999.

30. An excellent book about the increased weight of the financial sector is François Chesnais ed., *La mondialisation financière: Genèse, coût et enjeux*, Paris: Syros, 1996. See also R. Pollin & E. Zahrt, 'Expansionary policy for full employment in the United States: Retrospective on the 1960s and current period prospects', in Michie & Grieve Smith, *Employment and Economic Performance*; William Greider, *One World, Ready or Not: The Manic Logic of Global Capitalism*, New York: Simon & Schuster, 1997.

31. *Issues in Science and Technology*, summer 1991, p. 92, cited in Ruigrok & Van Tulder, *Logic of International Restructuring*, p. 143.

32. Daniele Archibugi & Jonathan Michie, 'The globalization of technology: A new taxonomy', *Cambridge Journal of Economics* no. 19 (1995).

33. Tom Nierop, 'De opkomst van de "Trillion-dollar-mega-netwerks"', *Business Topics* vol. 2 no. 1 (1995), p. 14.

34. 'Globalization bad for health, say UN agencies', *Financial Times*, 10 June 1999.

35. Barnet & Cavanagh, *Global Dreams*, pp. 16–17.

36. UNCTAD, *World Investment Report 1998*, pp.1–6.

37. Sources: Web sites of *Fortune* (www.fortune.com) and the World Bank (www.worldbank.org).

38. Tim Lang & Colin Hines, *The New Protectionism: Protecting the Future against Free Trade*, London: Earthscan, 1993, pp. 34–35.

39. Raymond Vernon, *In the Hurricane's Eye: The Troubled Prospects of Multinational Enterprises*, Cambridge: Harvard University Press, 1998, p. 10.

40. UNCTAD, *World Investment Report 1994: Transnational Corporations, Employment and the Workplace*, New York: UNCTAD, 1994, pp. 136–37.

41. *Economist*, 16 Sept. 1995, p. 27.

42. Kim Moody, 'Theses on the new GATT and the future of imperialism', *Solidarity Pre-Convention Bulletin* no. 6 (1994), p. 4.

43. François Chesnais, *La mondialisation du capital*, Paris: Syros, 1994, p. 15.

44. For mainstream critiques of exaggeratedly positive accounts of globalization, see, for example, Dani Rodrik, *Has*

Globalization Gone Too Far?, Washington: Institute for International Economics, 1997, and the same author's *New Global Economy*.

45. With mediocre results: see 'CIA muffs economic analysis: Agency is better at Communist foes than capital flows', *International Herald Tribune*, 16 Oct. 1995.
46. For criticisms of free-trade ideology from various points of view, see Ralph Nader et al., *The Case Against Free Trade: GATT, NAFTA, and the Globalization of Corporate Power*, San Francisco: Earth Island, 1993.
47. Tim Koechlin, 'A critical assessment of the debate over Nafta', *Review of Radical Political Economics* vol. 25 no. 3 (1993), p. 118.
48. Lang & Hines, *New Protectionism*, p. 50.
49. *Financial Times*, 11 Oct. 1995.
50. M. Hirsh, 'Capital wars', *Newsweek*, 3 Oct. 1994, p. 32.
51. *Financial Times*, 12 Aug. 1994.
52. Cited in Moisés Naím, 'Latin America the morning after', *Foreign Affairs*, July-Aug. 1995, p. 53.
53. Rodrik, *New Global Economy*, p. 151.
54. *Financial Times*, 12 Sept. 1995.
55. For the Netherlands this development has been documented by Arjen Van Witteloostuijn, *De anorexiastrategie: Over de gevolgen van saneren*, Amsterdam: De Arbeiderspers, 1999, who analyses it as an international trend towards 'Anglo-Saxonisation', leading towards 'macho management' and 'anorexia'.
56. R. Kuttner, 'The big snag in the global economy', *Business Week*, 1 Aug. 1994, p. 8.
57. Sociaal-Economische Raad, *Europa na Maastricht*, The Hague: SER, 1993, pp. 76–77.
58. J. Byrne, 'Why downsizing looks different today', *Business Week*, 10 Oct. 1994, p. 62.
59. Bernard Cassen, 'Technologie? Connais pas', *Le Monde Diplomatique*, July 1994, p. 22.
60. Charles Schwab & Claude Smadja, 'Power and policy: The new economic world order', *Harvard Business Review*, Nov.–Dec. 1994, p. 41.
61. W.J.M. Kickert, *NRC Handelsblad*, 19 Nov. 1994.
62. Adrie Duivesteijn, *De Volkskrant*, 23 Sept. 1995.
63. Sint, *NRC Handelsblad*, 19 Nov. 1994.
64. See Hirst & Thompson, *Globalization in Question*, and B. Sutcliffe, 'Freedom to move in the age of globalization', in Dean Baker et al., *Globalization and Progressive Economic Policy*, Cambridge: Cambridge University Press, 1998.

65. Henk Overbeek, 'Mondialisering en regionalisering: De wording van een Europese migratiepolitiek', *Migrantenstudies* no. 2 (1994), p. 68.

66. See Saskia Sassen, *The Global City: New York, London, Tokyo*, Princeton: Princeton University Press, 1991; Sassen, 'Immigration in Japan and the US: The weight of economic internationalization', in Hedwig Rudolph & Mirjana Morokvasic eds, *Bridging States and Markets: International Migration in the Early 1990s*, Berlin: Sigma, 1993; and Sassen, *Losing Control: Sovereignty in an Age of Globalization*, New York: Columbia University Press, 1996.

67. Overbeek, 'Modialisering en regionalisering', p. 71.

68. Overbeek, 'Modialisering en regionalisering', p. 80.

69. Arthur MacEwan, 'Globalisation and stagnation', in Miliband and Panitch, *Socialist Register 1994: Between Globalism and Nationalism*, London: Merlin Press, 1994, p. 130.

70. *Financial Times*, 8 Sept. 1995. For more detail and analysis on this subject, see Lawrence Mishel, Jared Bernstein & John Schmitt, *The State of Working America 1998–99*, Ithaca: Cornell University Press, 1999.

71. *NRC Handesblad*, 7 Sept. 1995.

72. UNCTAD, *Trade and Development Report 1997*, Geneva: UN, 1997, p. 5.

73. UNDP, *Human Development Report 1998*, New York: Oxford University Press, 1998, p. 29.

74. UNCTAD, *Trade and Development Report 1997*, pp. 7–8.

75. This same conclusion was drawn, surprisingly enough, by World Bank senior economist Lant Pritchett, who wrote that convergence 'just hasn't happened, isn't happening, and isn't going to happen without serious changes in economic policies in developing countries'. ('Forget convergence: Divergence past, present and future', *Finance & Development*, June 1995, pp. 40–43)

76. UNDP, *Human Development Report 1998*, p. 30.

77. Ruth Bandzak, 'The role of labor in post-socialist Hungary', *Journal of Economic Issues*, vol. 28 no. 2 (1994), p. 526.

78. Economic Intelligence Unit, *Financial Times*, 22 Aug. 1995.

79. K. Krumm et al., 'Transfers and the transition from central planning', *Finance & Development*, Sept. 1995, p. 30.

80. Irene van Staveren (*Economie: vrouwelijk; staathuiskunde. Econoom: mannelijk; staathuiskundige (Van Dale, 1976)*, Utrecht: Oikos, 1995) analyses the gender biases in the economy and in economics, while Sandra Whitworth ('Theory as exclusion: Gender and international political economy', in Richard Stubbs & Geoffrey Underhill eds, *Political Economy and the Changing Global Order*, Houndmills:

MacMillan, 1994) analyses women's exclusion from most studies of international relations.

81. Quotations in this section are all taken from Penelope Duggan & Heather Dashner eds, *Women's Lives in the New Global Economy*, Amsterdam: IIRE, 1994, pp. 7–10. See Maria Renzi, 'Globalization and adjustment policies in Central America', *LOLA Press* no. 9 (Nov. 1995–Mar. 1996), for the impact of globalization and economic crisis on Central American women.

82. David Morris, cited in Lang & Hines, *New Protectionism*, p. 59. Another example from the flower trade: there are flowers grown in Israel, flown to the international flower auction in Holland, and bought there for sale the next day in Israel – where they have to be flown back.

83. See F. Noakes, 'New trade regime "destroys democracy"', *Green Left Weekly*, 26 Oct. 1994, p. 9.

84. John Bellamy Foster, 'Waste away', *Dollars and Sense* no.195, Sept.–Oct. 1994, p. 7.

85. MacEwan, 'Globalisation and stagnation', p. 131.

86. See Noakes, 'New trade regime'.

87. S. Gill, 'The emerging world order and European change', in Miliband & Panitch, *Socialist Register 1992*, p. 168.

88. Ralph Miliband, *Socialism for a Sceptical Age*, Cambridge: Polity, 1994, p. 10.

89. See Anke Hintjens, 'A GATTastrophe for the Third World', and Vandana Shiva, 'The pillage of Third World diversity', in Toussaint & Drucker, *IMF/World Bank/WTO*.

90. See A. Kimbrell, 'The body enclosed: The commodification of human "parts"', *Ecologist* vol. 25 no. 4 (1995).

91. Taken in part from Ruigrok & Van Tulder, *Logic of International Restructuring*. See also Hirst & Thompson, *Globalization in Question*, and Paul Doremus et al., *The Myth of the Global Corporation*, Princeton: Princeton University Press, 1998.

92. *Het Financiele Dagblad*, 26 Sept. 1995.

93. Source: UNCTAD, *World Investment Report 1998*, p. 5.

94. See Walden Bello & Stephanie Rosenfeld, *Dragons in Distress: Asia's Miracle in Crisis*, San Francisco: Institute for Food and Development Policy, 1990, and Thomas Coutrot & Michel Husson, *Les destins du Tiers monde: Analyse, bilan et perspectives*, Luçon: Editions Nathan, 1993, pp. 105–37.

95. All these mechanisms – many more than the two discussed here – are reviewed in Toussaint & Drucker, *IMF/World Bank/WTO*.

96. Eric Toussaint, *Your Money or Your Life!: The Tyranny of Global Finance*, London: Pluto Press, 1998, pp. 93–94.

97. Augustín Papie (ex-member North-South Commission), PST, *Proyecto de Resolución sobre la Coyuntura Nacional*, Montevideo: PST, 1995, p. 5.

98. Barnet & Cavanaugh, *Global Dreams*, p. 427.

99. Ruigrok & Van Tulder, *Logic of International Restructuring*, p. 159. More recent studies, such as Hirst & Thompson, *Globalization in Question*, and Doremus et al., *Myth of the Global Corporation*, have reached similar conclusions.

100. 'The question then arises: why is anything still produced in the Netherlands at all? Why don't Dutch employers massively invest in Russia?' (Alfred Kleinknecht, *Heeft Nederland een loongolf nodig?: Een neo-Schumpeteriaans verhaal over bedrijfswinsten, werkelegenheid en export*, Amsterdam: VU, 1994, p. 7)

101. OECD economist Charles Oman, *Financial Times*, 6 Oct. 1995.

102. For example, the constantly repeated assertion that Dutch wage costs are far too high is open to many different criticisms:
   • It is wrong to look only or primarily at (direct and indirect) wage costs. Factors such as training, technical skills, infrastructure, product quality, product differentiation, service divisions, culture, proximity of sales outlets and many others are often more important. A recent report for the Employment Committee of the British House of Commons shows that Japanese companies hardly take low wage costs into account, or do not take them into account at all, in deciding whether to invest in England; Nissan's wage costs for example are less than 10 per cent of its total costs. (*Financial Times*, 11 Feb. 1994)
   • Higher wages generally reflect higher productivity, which can mean quite low labour costs per unit. Two researchers at the Technical University of Eindhoven concluded: 'The Netherlands is one of the most efficient countries in Europe. Multinationals' wage costs per unit of production are often the lowest in Western Europe.' (A. Van de Ven & A. Kok, 'De toekomst van de industrie', *Economisch Statistische Berichten*, 23 Mar. 1994, p. 264)

103. The manufacturer Giant decided for these reasons to move a bicycle factory from Taiwan to the high-wage Dutch town of Lelystad, for example (*Het Parool*, 7 Oct. 1995). Ruigrok & Van Tulder, *Logic of International Restructuring*, pp. 174–200, distinguish seven different ways in which companies internationalise, ranging from setting up a screwdriver factory to 'biregionalisation', 'glocalisation' and globalization.

104. Hobsbawm, 'Guessing about global change' *International Labor and Working-Class History, no. 47* (1995), p. 43.

105. Steven Vogel, *Freer Markets, More Rules: Regulatory Reform in Advanced Industrial Countries,* Ithaca: Cornell University Press, 1996, p. 3.
106. 'The illusion of French liberalism', *European,* 26 May 1994.
107. *Economist,* 6 Aug. 1994.
108. Ann May & Kurt Stephenson, 'Women and the great retrenchment: The political economy of gender in the 1980s', *Journal of Economic Issues* vol. 28 no. 2 (1994), p. 535.
109. See Murray, 'The internationalization of capital'.
110. Free-market champion Ronald Reagan in particular spent billions to nationalise the problem-plagued Continental Illinois Bank (Steven Solomon, *The Confidence Game: How Unelected Central Bankers Are Governing the Changed World Economy,* New York: Simon & Schuster, 1995, pp. 171–72). An editorial in *Business Week* (2 Oct. 1995) also noted with satisfaction after the Japanese government intervened to ward off several banks' bankruptcy that after years of hesitation the Japanese Ministry of Finance had finally published a plan to use public money in the event of future bank failures.
111. See Linda Weiss, *The Myth of the Powerless State,* Ithaca: Cornell University Press, 1998.

Chapter 2

1. Marcel van Dam, *De opmars der dingen,* Putten: Balans, 1994, pp. 9–10.
2. C. Adam, 'Internationalization and integration of financial and capital markets', in Amnon Levy-Livermore, *Handbook on the Globalization of the World Economy,* Cheltenham: Edward Elgar, 1998, p. 559.
3. Charles-Albert Michelet, *Le capitalisme mondial,* Paris: Quadrige/PUF, 1998.
4. Andrew Walter, *World Power and World Money,* New York: Harvester Wheatsheaf, 1993, pp. 199–210.
5. Walter, *World Power and World Money,* p. 202.
6. Mainstream economists are unable to explain the changes in the world, let alone develop tools with which people could bring them under better control. See Paul Ormerod, *The Death of Economics,* London: Faber and Faber, 1994.
7. Arguments of this kind are often full of glaring contradictions. Take for example Frits Bolkestein, former leader of the right-wing Dutch governing party VVD and now a member of the European Commission. In his book *Het heft in handen* (Amsterdam: Prometheus, 1995) he repeatedly condemns 1970s radicals, as well as anyone whose opinions differ from

his own, for their outdated assumption that society can be changed. But Bolkestein himself makes that same assumption. In response to the idea that unemployment is an unsolvable problem, he writes: 'But there is no such thing as historical determinism. Nothing that happens is unavoidable. We are standing by and watching this; we are the ones who are letting it happen.' Whereupon he argues for lowering the minimum wage, making layoffs easier, and so forth and so on. Now if that is not an argument for changing society – in the direction that Bolkestein wants it to be changed – then I do not know what is. However hard he works to portray his own economic ideas as unavoidable, he ultimately cannot avoid revealing that we are free to choose a different direction.

8.   An offshore market is one where financial transactions take place in foreign currencies in order to serve non-residents. Banking in these markets can be attractive thanks to lower tax rates and less control and regulation. A number of small countries such as Bermuda, the Cayman Islands, Monaco, Hong Kong, Luxemburg and Lichtenstein have built up extensive offshore financial centres.

       Eurodollars are currencies that are held by individuals and institutions outside the issuing country. The BIS describes Eurodollars as dollars obtained by banks operating outside the US, mostly in the form of deposits (but also to a certain extent in the form of swaps for other currencies in dollars), and lent out in turn to non-bank borrowers elsewhere in the world. While the first Eurodollars were dollars in a North American bank held by the Moscow-based Narodny Bank whose London office lent them out elsewhere in Western Europe, Eurodollars do not in fact have to be dollars or held in Europe. Today all possible Eurocurrencies are being traded all over the world (G. Bannock, R. Baxter & E. Davis, *The Penguin Dictionary of Economics*, London: Penguin, 1992, p. 138; G. Bannock & W. Manser, *The Penguin International Dictionary of Finance*, London: Penguin, 1995).

9.   Eric Helleiner, 'Explaining the globalization of financial markets: Bringing the states back in', *Review of International Political Economy* vol. 2 no. 2 (1995).

10.   Helleiner, 'Freeing money: Why have states been more willing to liberalize capital controls than trade barriers?', *Policy Sciences* no. 27 (1994), p. 310, points out that neoliberal ideas were gaining more and more of a following in the industrialised countries in the 1970s and 1980s, and that the US decision in the early 1970s to liberalise capital flows was due in part to growing neoliberal influence.

11. Walter, *World Power and World Money*, p. 208; Helleiner, 'Freeing money', p. 308.
12. Steven Solomon, *The Confidence Game: How Unelected Central Bankers Are Governing the Changed World Economy*, New York: Simon & Schuster, 1995.
13. Ulrich Duchrow, *Alternatives to Global Capitalism: Drawn from Biblical History, Designed for Political Action*, Utrecht: International Books, 1995, p. 102.
14. Michie, 'Introduction', in Michie & Grieve Smith, *Managing the Global Economy*, Oxford: Oxford University Press, 1995, p. xxvi.
15. See François Chesnais, *Tobin or not Tobin?: Une taxe internationale sur le capital*, Paris: L'Esprit Frappeur, 1999.
16. Michel Camdessus, 'The IMF way to open capital accounts', *Wall Street Journal*, 29 Sept. 1995.
17. Solomon, *Confidence Game*, p. 111.
18. Ruth Kelly, who writes on economics for the London *Guardian* , says that moving towards official registration of all transactions should be a priority ('Derivatives: A growing threat to the international financial system', in Michie & Grieve Smith, *Managing the Global Economy*, pp. 224–29).
19. Kelly, 'Derivatives', p. 227.
20. Manfred Bienefeld, 'Capitalism and the nation state in the dog days of the twentieth century', in Ralph Miliband and Leo Panitch eds, *Socialist Register 1994: Between Globalism and Nationalism*, London: Merlin Press, 1994, pp. 101–02.
21. Bienefeld, 'Capitalism and the nation state', pp. 102–03.
22. See in particular Christopher Freeman, 'The economics of technical change', *Cambridge Journal of Economics* no. 18 (1994), p. 483.
23. Peter Dicken, *Global Shift: Industrial Change in a Turbulent World*, London: Harper & Row, 1986, pp. 106–7.
24. B. Bimber, 'Three faces of technological determinism', in Merritt Roe Smith & Leo Marx eds, *Does Technology Drive History?: The Dilemma of Technological Determinism*, Cambridge: MIT Press, 1995, p. 95.

Chapter 3

1. Frits Bolkestein, *NRC Handelsblad*, 29 Nov. 1994.
2. Eric Hobsbawm, *Age of Extremes: The Short Twentieth Century, 1914–1991*, London: Michael Joseph, 1994, p. 87.
3. The US Federal Reserve's Open Market Committee, whose monetary policy has a direct impact on economic trends, managed to predict GNP growth more or less well in only a

third of the cases between 1980 and 1994, for example (*Business Week,* 25 Sept. 1995). The economist E. Westerhout concluded at one point that the Dutch Central Planning Bureau hardly did better on average than anyone could do by extrapolating last year's trends to next year ('De kwaliteit van CPB-voorspellingen', *Economisch Statistische Berichten,* 12 Sept. 1990). This is extremely annoying for economists and econometrists who claim to be able to make good prognoses from their models. 'Predicting is difficult, especially the future,' is one joking comment. Still less flattering is the definition of an economist as 'someone can who explain to you today why the prediction he or she made the day before yesterday didn't come true yesterday'.

4. Daniel Bensaïd has written two outstanding books on Marx's relevance today: *La discordance des temps: Essais sur les crises, les classes, l'histoire,* Paris: Editions de la Passion, 1995, and *Marx l'intempestif: Grandeurs et misères d'une aventure critique (XIXe-XXe siècles),* Paris: Fayard, 1995.

5. See Christian Barsoc, *Les rouages du capitalisme: Eléments d'analyse économique marxiste,* Paris: La Brèche, 1994. In this chapter and in Chapter 4 the use of a number of Marxist economic concepts is unavoidable. As far as possible, the terms are described or defined simply (sometimes *too* simply). Readers who find this insufficient or would like to know more can consult one of the many existing introductions to Marxist economics, such as Ernest Mandel, *Introduction to Marxist Economic Theory,* New York: Pathfinder, 1970, or Duncan Foley, *Understanding Capital: Marx's Economic Theory,* Cambridge: Harvard University Press, 1986.

   Here is a brief explanation of the concepts used in this section:

   In Part III of *Das Kapital* Marx explains that surplus-value is divided into profit, interest and land rent. In this context we ignore this, and define the rate of profit as equal to profits divided by invested constant plus variable capital: $s/c+v$.

   If we divided both the numerator and denominator of this fraction by v, then we have $(s/v)/[(c/v)+1]$. Written in this way the formula offers some insight into possible changes in the rate of profit.

   s/v is the rate of surplus-value or rate of exploitation. It indicates the ratio between that part of value produced that the employer appropriates and that part that is paid out as wages. Implication: if wages rise at the expense of profits, then in principle - if no contrary tendencies are at work - the rate of profit falls.

c/v is the organic composition of capital. It indicates the ratio between capital invested in machines and raw materials and capital invested in labour power. Implication: if the organic composition of capital rises, for instance through automation, then in principle - if no contrary tendencies are at work - the rate of profit falls.

6. The Russian Parvus and the Dutchmen Van Gelderen and De Wolff were among those who wrote about long waves before Kondratiev. See Jaap van Duijn, *De longe golf in de economie*, Assen: Van Gorcum, 1979, pp. 30–32, and Frank Kalshoven, *Over marxistische economie in Nederland, 1883–1939*, Amsterdam: Thesis Publishers, 1993, p. 119.

7. In the same vein long waves were described in a 1978 issue of the *Citibank Monthly Economic Letter* as a myth spread by people who believe in a mystical unfolding of history (Joshua Goldstein, *Long Cycles, Prosperity and War in the Modern Age*, New Haven: Yale University Press, 1988, pp. 21–22).

8. Ernest Mandel, *Long Waves of Capitalist Development: A Marxist Interpretation*, London: Verso, 1995, p. 97.

9. Goldstein, *Long Cycles*, p. 62.

10. Source: Barsoc, *Les rouages du capitalisme*, p. 53.

11. Source: World Bank data cited in Harry Magdoff, 'Globalization: To what end?', in Ralph Miliband & Leo Panitich eds, *Socialist Register 1992: New World Order?*, London: Merlin Press, 1992, p. 48.

12. Source: J. Eatwell, 'The international origins of unemployment', in Jonathan Michie & John Grieve Smith eds, *Managing the Global Economy*, Oxford: Oxford University Press, 1995, p. 276. The Dutch figures have been calculated on the basis of data from the Dutch Central Planning Bureau.

13. Hobsbawm, *Age of Extremes*, p. 87n.

14. This schematic classification of the major currents in the discussion is borrowed from Goldstein, *Long Cycles*, pp. 23–39. Other theories were developed in which various explanations were combined.

15. This debate between Kondratiev and Trotsky reflected deep differences of opinion within Marxism, which were already under discussion before the long-wave debate broke out and that concern many things besides long waves. It was related to the discussion between Kautsky and Lenin over capitalist stability or instability and the political conclusions that flowed from it for the strategy of the workers' movement: Kondratiev tended towards Kautsky's conservative position while Trotsky shared Lenin's revolutionary optimism. (Goldstein, *Long Cycles*, p. 31)

16. This classification is taken from Goldstein (*Long Cycles*, p. 40).

17. In works published in English in 1978, 1980, 1992 and 1995, all listed in the bibliography.
18. Phillip O'Hara, 'An institutionalist review of long wave theories: Schumpeterian innovation modes of regulation and social structures of accumulation', *Journal of Economic Issues* vol. 28 no. 2 (1994), p. 496.
19. Mandel, *Long Waves*, p. 105.
20. Barsoc, *Les rouages du capitalisme*, p. 52.
21. Mandel, 'The international debate on long waves of capitalist development: An intermediary balance sheet', in Alfred Kleinknecht, Mandel and Immanuel Wallerstein eds, *New Findings in Long-Wave Research*, New York: St Martin's Press, 1992, pp. 327–29.
22. Karl Marx, *Capital*, Harmondsworth: Penguin, 1981, vol. 3, pp. 317–79. See also Foley, *Understanding Capital*, pp. 125–41; Geert Reuten, 'Accumulation of capital and the foundation of the tendency of the rate of profit to fall', *Cambridge Journal of Economics* vol. 15 (1991); and Reuten & Michael Williams, *Value-Form and the State: The Tendencies of Accumulation and the Determination of Economic Policy in Capitalist Society*, London: Routledge, 1989, pp. 116–39.
23. Against the backdrop of his explanation of falling rates of profit, explaining periodic increases in the rate of profit was also the crucial problem for Marx (see, for example, Geert Reuten, 'The notion of tendency in Marx's 1894 Law of profit', in Fred Moseley & Martha Campbell eds, *New Investigations of Marx's Method*, Highland Park: Humanities Press, 1997).
24. 'One of the main reasons that there have been so many misunderstandings about Marx's economic theory is precisely that by misunderstanding his method of operating at successively different levels of abstraction ... , many of his commentators and critics have attributed to him a mechanical correlation between these basic variables, which is in contradiction not only to the internal logic of his system but also to what he explicitly stated on the subject' (Mandel, *Long Waves*, p. 10).
25. As set out in footnote 5 (above), the rate of profit (s/c+v) can be reformulated as (s/v)/[(c/v)+1]. This formula makes it simple to see how fluctuations in the organic composition of capital (c/v) – shifts in the relationship between constant and variable capital, for example, as a result of automation – and fluctuations in the rate of exploitation (s/v) – shifts in the relationship between profits and wages, for example, if profits rise because wages fall – determine the development of the rate of profit. Changes in the time necessary for production and circulation change capital's turnover time, which also affects

the rate of profit: if invested capital is available more quickly for reinvestment, it can be invested more often and thus generate more profits.

26. Mandel, *Long Waves*, p. 37.

27. This schema, which has many similarities to that of the French Regulation School, is borrowed from Barsoc, *Les rouages du capitalisme*, pp. 54–55.

28. Mandel, *Long Waves*, p. 76.

29. A. Glyn, A. Hughes, A. Lipietz & A. Singh, 'The rise and fall of the Golden Age', in Stephan Marglin & Juliet Schor eds, *The Golden Age of Capitalism: Reinterpreting the Postwar Experience*, Oxford: Clarendon Press, 1990, p. 95.

30. L. Stoleru, *L'Equilibre et la croissance économiques*, Paris: Dunod, 1970, cited in Mandel, *La Crise, 1974–1982: Les Faits, Leur Interprétation Marxiste*, Paris: Flammarion, 1982, p. 8. (The English version of Mandel's book, *The Second Slump: A Marxist Analysis of Recession in the Seventies*, London: NLB, 1978, is an earlier one and does not include this citation.)

31. Hobsbawm, *Age of Extremes*, p. 260.

32. Dani Rodrik, *The New Global Economy and Developing Countries: Making Openness Work*, Washington: Johns Hopkins University Press, 1999, p. 68.

33. See Mandel, *Late Capitalism*, London: Verso, 1978, and Ralph Miliband & Leo Panitch eds, *Socialist Register 1992: New World Order?*, London: Merlin Press, 1992.

34. See Mandel, *Late Capitalism*, pp. 184–208 and 248–73.

35. Reflation is a macroeconomic policy in which demand is pumped up in order to reduce unemployment.

36. Source: Glyn et al., 'Rise and fall', p. 42.

37. Source: Glyn et al., 'Rise and fall', p. 44.

38. Mandel, *Long Waves*, p. 18.

39. Barsoc, *Les rouages du capitalisme*, p. 56.

40. Mandel, *Long Waves*, p. 112.

41. Robert Boyer, *The Convergence Hypothesis Revisited: Globalization but Still the Century of Nations?*, Paris: CEPREMAP-CNRS-EHESS, 1993, p. 23.

42. Anton Hemerijck & Wieger Bakker, 'De pendule van perspectief: Convergentie en divergentie in het denken over de verzorgingsstaat', in Gottfried Engbersen, Hemerijck & Bakker, *Zorgen in het Europese huis: Verkenningen over de grenzen van nationale verzorgingsstaten*, Amsterdam: Boom, 1994, pp. 23–24.

43. Maarten van Bottenburg, *'Aan de Arbeid!': In de wandelgangen van de Stichting van de Arbeid, 1945–1995*, Amsterdam: Bert Bakker, 1995, p. 50. No wonder that Stikker insisted that the

unions launch the Foundation for Labour: 'The plan must for the most part be launched by the leaders of the workers' movement; it must be an outcome that they bring about – then this plan will achieve the needed political significance' (Van Bottenburg, p. 39).

44.   J. Roebroek, 'De confessionele verzorgingsstaat', in Kees van Kersbergen, Paul Lucardie & Hans-Martien ten Napel eds, *Geloven in macht: De christen-democratie in Nederland*, Amsterdam: Het Spinhuis, 1993, p. 183.

45.   Glyn et al., 'Rise and fall', p. 39.

46.   Source: Glyn et al., 'Rise and fall', p. 47.

47.   Source: Glyn et al., 'Rise and fall', p. 44.

48.   Source: Glyn et al., 'Rise and fall', p. 47.

49.   Leo Panitch & Ralph Miliband, 'The new world order and the socialist agenda', in Miliband & Panitich eds, *Socialist Register 1992*, p. 10.

50.   Mandel, *Long Waves*, pp. 64–75.

51.   Mandel comments himself that this is a controversial proposition, particularly (but not only) among Marxist economists: 'In *Late Capitalism* we addressed a challenge to our colleagues that has not yet been taken up. Let those who deny the validity of the tendency of the organic composition of capital to rise cite an example of a single branch of industry in which labor costs today constitute a higher proportion of total costs than they did seventy-five, fifty, or forty years ago. It will be difficult to find such an example, not to mention discovering a general trend in that direction. For what is semiautomation all about if not labor-saving-biased technical progress?' (*Long Waves*, p. 65)

52.   A company must not only create as much profit as possible in the production process, but also 'realise' the profit contained in the goods produced by selling the products. If for example buying power declines or there is overproduction, it can become more and more difficult to sell the goods: these are 'difficulties of realisation'.

Chapter 4

1.   William Bridges, 'The end of the job', *Fortune*, 19 Sept. 1994, p. 46.

2.   Walter Heller, *New Dimensions of Political Economy*, New York: W.W. Norton & Co., 1967, p. 104; Wilhelm Weber & Hubert Weiss, *Konjunktuur- und Beschäftigungstheorie*, Cologne: Kiepenheuer & Witsch, 1967, p. 14; Roy Harrod, *Money*, London: St Martin's Press, 1969, pp. 188, 190, all cited in

Ernest Mandel, *La crise 1974–1982: Les faits, leur interprétation marxiste,* Paris: Flammarion, 1982, pp. 7–8n1 (citations not included in the English version: Ernest Mandel, *The Second Slump: A Marxist Analysis Of Recession in the Seventies,* London: NLB, 1978). Mandel notes that Marxists 'had foreseen the crisis and predicted its outbreak, almost to the exact date' (*The Second Slump,* p. 9).

3.   Mandel, *The Second Slump,* p. 15.
4.   Source: 'Annex' in OECD, *Economic Outlook* no. 55 (1994).
5.   Bernard Connolly, *The Rotten Heart of Europe: The Dirty War for Europe's Money,* London: Faber & Faber, 1995, pp. 20–21.
6.   *NRC Handelsblad,* 30 Sept. 1995.
7.   John Holloway, 'The abyss opens: The rise and fall of Keynesianism', in Werner Bonefeld & John Holloway eds, *Global Capital, National States and the Politics of Money,* London: St Martin's Press, 1995, p. 9.
8.   For a comparable analysis, see Harry Shutt, *The Trouble with Capitalism,* London: Zed Books, 1998.
9.   The chief losers in high inflation as it existed in the late 1970s are financial institutions and the rich, the ones who hold most of the fixed-rate, money-denominated assets (particularly bonds). They suffer the most if real interest rates go down because of inflation or even become negative, as was briefly the case in the late 1970s; and they are the ones who benefit the most from a crusade against inflation.
10. G. Millman, *The Vandals' Crown: How Rebel Currency Traders Overthrew the World's Central Banks,* New York: Free Press, 1995, p. 170.
11. Central bankers' and economists' main argument for the greatest possible independence for central banks is directly linked to this fight against inflation. Briefly and schematically, their argument is that independent central banks are better able to resist pressure from governments that want to use monetary policy for their own electoral purposes and from people who want to raise their living standards more quickly than their countries can afford. Defenders of autonomous central banks acknowledge that this puts very considerable power in the hands of unelected functionaries. But the disadvantage of this 'democratic deficit' is supposedly outweighed by the economic prosperity that central bank independence leads to (according to their theory).
12. Mandel, *La crise,* p. 233.
13. Western banks, who had had to find something to do with their 'petrodollars', had among other things gladly lent to credit-hungry Third World governments.

14. See Steven Solomon, *The Confidence Game: How Unelected Central Bankers Are Governing the Changed World Economy*, New York: Simon & Schuster, 1995, pp. 193–273, for a description of the emergence of this debt crisis, the potential consequences for hundreds of Western banks, and the measures taken by the main industrialised countries' central banks and the IMF to prevent an international crisis of the financial system.

15. *NRC Handelsblad*, 30 Sept. 1995.

16. Mandel, *La crise*, p. 200.

17. On these developments, often referred to as 'Toyotism' and 'Japanisation', see Tony Smith, *Lean Production: A Capitalist Utopia?*, Amsterdam: IIRE, 1994, and Hans Boot, 'Management-filosofieën – van school tot bedrijf: De tijd van onderschatting is voorbij', *Solidariteit* no. 68 (1995).

18. For a description of this change from a neoliberal point of view, see David Henderson, *The Changing Fortunes of Economic Liberalism: Yesterday, Today and Tomorrow*, London: Institute of Economic Affairs, 1998.

19. Gottfried Engbersen, 'De weg naar Amonia?: Armoederegimes en levenskansen', in Engbersen, Anton Hemerijck & Wieger Bakker, *Zorgen in het Europese huis: Verkenningen over de grenzen van nationale verzorgingsstaten*, Amsterdam: Boom, 1994.

20. ' ... The 1976 Nobel Prize for Economics awarded to Milton Friedman was the symbol of the "anti-Keynesian counter-revolution" that has occurred in bourgeois economic ideology. This "counter-revolution" reflects a shift in the socio-economic priorities of the capitalist class both materially and in terms of class struggle.

'Indeed, the official spokesman of the international bourgeoisie, as well as bourgeois representatives of academic science, are not mincing words in this regard. Professor Karl Brunner, a leading Swiss monetarist now living in the United States, has asserted: "If we want to eliminate inflation there will be a price to pay, and that price is unemployment. Unemployment is therefore the social cost of putting an end to inflation. And don't come and tell me there's another way out, because it's not true." One of the world's leading monetarists, the recently deceased Professor Harry G. Johnson, expressed himself no less coarsely, "The answer [to inflation] depends ... in the long run ... on the will of society to turn away from the Welfare State."' (*Tendances/Trends*, 8 Sept. 1976, and *Banker*, Aug. 1975, both cited in Mandel, *Second Slump*, pp. 86–87)

21. Simon Clarke, *Keynesianism, Monetarism and the Crisis of the State,* Aldershot: Edward Elgar, 1988, p. 1.

22. 'The turnabout of academic economics ... *was essentially a product of a basic switch in class struggle priorities of the capitalist class ...*

   'When we pass from an expansionist long wave to a depressive long wave, it is no longer possible to assure full employment, to eradicate poverty, to extend social security, to assure a steady (if modest) increase in real income for the wage earners. At that point the fight to restore the rate of profit through a strong upswing in the rate of surplus value (i.e., the rate of exploitation of the working class) becomes the top priority.

   'The monetarists' "anti-Keynesian counterrevolution" in the realm of academic economics is nothing but the ideological expression of this changed priority.' (Mandel, *Long Waves,* pp. 77–78)

23. Holloway, 'The abyss opens', pp. 29–30.

24. Francis Fukuyama, *The End of History and the Last Man,* London: Penguin, 1992.

25. See Eric Helleiner, 'Freeing money: Why have states been more willing to liberalize capital controls than trade barriers?', *Policy Sciences* no. 27 (1994).

26. R. Meidner, 'Why did the Swedish model fail?', in Ralph Miliband & Leo Panitch eds, *Socialist Register 1993: Real Problems, False Solutions,* London: Merlin Press, 1993, p. 226.

27. Samir Amin, 'De nieuwe wereldoverheersing van het kapitalisme: Problemen en vooruitzichten', *Vlaams Marxistisch Tijdschrift* vol. 28 no. 3 (1994), pp. 34–35.

28. See Ernest Mandel, *Late Capitalism,* London: Verso, 1978.

29. See François Chesnais, *La mondialisation du capital,* Paris: Syros, 1994, pp. 22–23.

30. *Business Week,* 23 Jan. 1995.

31. See Robert Boyer & Jean-Pierre Durand, *L'après-fordisme,* Paris: Syros, 1998. For a more detailed account of Toyotist management techniques, see Tony Smith, *Lean Production: A Capitalist Utopia?,* Amsterdam: IIRE, 1994.

32. For a more detailed account, see Thomas Coutrot's excellent book, *L'entreprise néo-liberale: Nouvelle utopie capitaliste?,* Paris: La Découverte, 1998.

33. See Paul Krugman, *The Return of Depression Economics,* New York: W.W. Norton, 1999.

34. For such proposals, see, for example, the memoranda published by the Network of European Economists for an Alternative Economic Policy: 'Full employment, social cohesion and equity for Europe: Alternatives to competitive

austerity' (May 1997) and 'Full employment, solidarity and sustainability in Europe: Old challenges, new opportunities for economic policy' (Dec. 1998).

35. See Gilbert Achcar, *L'empire et l'argent: Essai sur les fondements de la stratégie impériale des Etats-Unis d'Amérique*, Paris: University of Paris VIII: Saint-Denis, 1993; Achcar, 'The strategic triad: The United States, Russia and China', *New Left Review* no. 228 (Mar./Apr. 1998); Robert Brenner, 'The economics of global turbulence', *New Left Review* no. 229 (1998); Peter Gowan, *The Globalization Gamble: The Dollar/Wall Street Regime and Its Consequences*, n.p., 1998.

36. Gresham's Law says: 'Bad money drives out good money.'

37. W. Sengenberger & F. Wilkinson, 'Globalization and labour standards', in Jonathan Michie & John Grieve Smith eds, *Managing the Global Economy*, Oxford: Oxford University Press, 1995, p. 129.

38. C. Farrell, 'Riding high: Corporate America now has an edge over its global rivals', *Business Week*, 16 Oct. 1995, p. 42.

39. A. van Zweeden, 'Verbroken evenwicht', *NRC Handelsblad*, 30 Sept. 1995.

40. For capital as a whole, not necessarily for each individual employer, of course.

41. Raymond Vernon, *In the Hurricane's Eye: The Troubled Prospects of Multinational Enterprises*, Cambridge: Harvard University Press, 1998, warns of a possible political backlash against multinationals as a result of globalization and their increased power.

42. See David Harvey, *The Condition of Postmodernity*, Oxford: Basil Blackwell, 1990, p. 124.

43. For a more detailed analysis see in particular the work of the French Marxist economist Michel Husson, 'L'école de la régulation après la crise', in Farida Sebaï & Carlo Vercellone eds, *Ecole de la régulation et critique de la raison économique*, Paris: L'Harmattan, 1994.

44. Source: Various OECD *Economic Outlooks*.

45. Source: Various OECD *Economic Outlooks*.

46. See Sengenberger & Wilkinson, 'Globalization and labour standards', for an account of the negative implications of growing income inequality for economic growth.

47. David Bogler, 'Big share of the profits', *Financial Times*, 24 Jan. 2000.

48. '21st Century capitalism: How nations and industries will compete in the emerging global economy – part 2', *Business Week*, 19 Dec. 1994, pp. 56–7. A trade union activist at Unilever in Rotterdam told me a story that is quite relevant here. He had explained to the president of a trade union feder-

ation that organises workers in the Unilever factory in Sri Lanka why in a very poor country like Sri Lanka Unilever, instead of producing food for the great majority of the population that has little or nothing to eat, makes the luxury product ice cream. The reason is that a multinational like Unilever focuses everywhere on the minority that has money to spend.

49. See, for example, *The Economist*, 5 Nov. 1994.

50. The importance of globalization for the restructuring of capitalism can be explained in yet another way, by going back to the determinants of the rate of profit mentioned in Chapter 3. In the previous section we mentioned that profits have been gradually rising since the early 1980s. Why is this?

1. Clearly, the rate of exploitation has increased as a result of the fact that real wages have lagged behind productivity increases, the fact that expenditures on social services (postponed wages) have declined, and increased flexibility (more production with fewer workers). In this chapter we have explained the role that globalization has played in bringing all this about. Globalization also lowers the chances that full employment will re-emerge in the future and exert a downward pressure on the rate of exploitation, since global sourcing and transfers of production to other parts of the world mean that an increasing share of the world's unemployed – according to the UN, 30 per cent of the world's population – is available in practice as a reserve army of labour. The labour market may be scarcely globalised at all, but because multinationals can invest more easily around the world, buy their parts around the world and delocalise production (or threaten to do so), the labour market is becoming more global despite the relative immobility of labour. Dani Rodrik, *Has Globalization Gone Too Far?*, Washington: Institute for International Economics, 1997, points to this greater elasticity of demand for labour as a consequence of globalization.

2. Globalization of the financial sector, deregulation and liberalisation, and the decreased controlling and regulatory role of national states have made it possible for capital's turnover time to decrease.

3. Among the forces that, according to Marx, *can* counteract the tendential fall of the rate of profit, one in particular is very pronounced because of globalization. Capitalism's area of domination and influence has spread enormously since the early 1980s and, thanks to globalization, multinationals, investors and speculators can spread their production, sales, investments and speculations around the world.

51.   For an analysis of the rise of neoliberalism, the interests
      behind it and the networks and structures that they use, see
      Hans Overbeek & Kees van der Pijl, 'Restructuring capital
      and restructuring hegemoney: Neo-liberalism and the
      unmaking of the post-war order', in Overbeek ed.,
      *Restructuring Hegemony in the Global Political Economy: The Rise
      of Transnational Neo-Liberalism in the 1980s*, London:
      Routledge, 1993.
52.   In a stimulating and thoroughly documented analysis, Robert
      Brenner also reaches sceptical conclusions about the possi-
      bility of a new boom: 'The perpetuation and exacerbation of
      longer-term trends toward international over-capacity and
      over-production seems more likely than their transcendence.'
      ('The economics of global turbulence', p. 261)

Chapter 5

1.   *Financial Times*, 20 Dec. 1994.
2.   Paul Krugman, *The Return of Depression Economics*, New York:
     W.W. Norton, 1999, p. 16
3.   See Tony Smith, *Lean Production: A Capitalist Utopia?*,
     Amsterdam: IIRE, 1994. This is definitely not a linear devel-
     opment. There are new sectors, particularly the service sector,
     in which Fordist and Taylorist methods are only now being
     introduced.
4.   See Philip Klein, 'A reassessment of institutionalist-main-
     stream relations', *Journal of Economic Issues* vol. 28 no. 1
     (1994), p. 197.
5.   'Nostalgia for the stable, postwar compromise of the national
     welfare state is ... misplaced and unrealistic. The historic
     compromise was based on the stable international order of the
     Cold War years. The new, post-1989 international order must
     be characterised above all as disordered. The national
     building blocks on which Keynes and Beveridge's welfare state
     rested were a homogeneous society, full employment regu-
     lated by Keynesian macroeconomic policy, a Fordist structure
     of production, centrally organised and very institutionalised
     interest groups of labour and capital, a self-confident inter-
     ventionist state and the traditional family. None of these
     preconditions can be met today. Leaving aside the tremen-
     dous changes in the structure of production, Keynesian
     policies of demand stimulation are unworkable in a world of
     global competition and free capital markets. With the loss of
     its economic frontiers, the nation-state has lost its sovereignty
     over monetary and fiscal policy. This limits to a major extent

the national welfare state's capacity to correct markets – even within an integrated European political economy. Under the deflationary criteria of the European Monetary Union, Keynesian policy prescriptions are not very realistic.' (Anton Hemerijk & Wieger Bakker, 'De pendule van perspectief: Convergentie en divergentie in het denken over de verzorgingsstaat', in Gottfried Engbersen, Anton Hemerijck & Wieger Bakker, *Zorgen in het Europese huis: Verkenningen over de grenzen van nationale verzorgingsstaten*, Amsterdam: Boom, 1994, pp. 50–51)

6. Stephan Marglin & A. Bhaduri, 'Profit squeeze and Keynesian theory', in Stephan Marglin & Juliet Schor eds, *The Golden Age of Capitalism: Reinterpreting the Postwar Experience*, Oxford: Clarendon Press, 1991, p. 184.

7. See, for example, Dani Rodrik, *The New Global Economy and Developing Countries: Making Openness Work*, Washington: Johns Hopkins University Press, 1999.

8. See Charles Tilly, 'Globalization threatens labor's rights', *International Labor and Working-Class History* no. 47 (1995), p. 5.

9. For example, Immanuel Wallerstein, 'Declining states, declining rights?', *International Labor and Working-Class History* no. 47 (1995), p. 26.

10. See J. Breman, 'Een laat-kapitalistisch manifest', *Volkskrant*, 7 Oct. 1995.

11. Ishac Diwan & Ana Revenga, 'The outlook for workers in the 21st century', *Finance and Development*, Sept. 1995, p. 11.

12. A number of earlier crises and near-crises are described in Steven Solomon, *The Confidence Game: How Unelected Central Bankers Are Governing the Changed World Economy*, New York: Simon & Schuster, 1995.

13. *Economist*, 12 June 1999.

14. UNDP, *Human Development Report 1999*, New York: Oxford University Press, 1999, p. 4.

15. Barry Eichengreen, *Toward a New International Financial Architecture: A Practical Post-Asia Agenda*, Washington: Institute for International Economics, 1999, p. 9.

16. For a description of the Chiapas rebellion and an analysis of the background to it, see, for example, John Ross, *Rebellion from the Roots: Indian Uprising in Chiapas*, Monroe: Common Courage Press, 1995.

17. *Veja*.

18. *Business Week*, 13 Feb. 1995.

19. Willem Buiter, *International Herald Tribune*, 2 Feb. 1995.

20. Eichengreen, *Toward a New International Financial Architecture*, p. 9.

21. Anne Krueger, 'Trade policy and economic development: How we learn', *American Economic Review* vol. 87 no. 1 (1997), pp. 9–10.

22. J. Sachs, 'Power unto itself', *Financial Times*, 11 Dec. 1997, p. 11.

23. Krugman, *Return of Depression Economics*, p. 103.

24. See George Soros, *The Crisis of Global Capitalism: Open Society Endangered*, Boston: Little, Brown, 1998.

25. Krugman, *Return of Depression Economics*, pp. 112, 117.

26. Walden Bello, 'The end of the Asian miracle', *Nation*, 12–19 Jan. 1998, p. 20.

27. See, for example, Samir Amin, 'De nieuwe wereldoverheersing van het kapitalisme: Problemen en vooruitzichten', *Vlaams Marxistisch Tijdschrift* vol. 28 no. 3 (1994).

28. A. Glyn & B. Sutcliffe, 'Global but leaderless?: The new capitalist order', in Ralph Miliband & Leo Panitch eds, *Socialist Register 1992: New World Order?*, London: Merlin Press, 1992, p. 93. Henk Overbeek pointed out to me that the same was true of Karl Kautsy in his article about 'ultra-imperialism', published in August 1914 in *Die Neue Zeit*.

29. Simon Clarke, 'The global accumulation of capital and the periodisation of the capitalist state form', in Werner Bonefeld, Richard Gunn & Kosmo Psychopedis eds, *Open Marxism I*, London: Pluto Press, 1992, pp. 146–47.

30. See, for example, *Economist*, 11 Dec. 1999.

31. See, for example, Walden Bello, *Focus on Trade* no. 42 (Dec. 1999), distributed by email.

32. James Tobin, 'A proposal for international monetary reform', *Eastern Economic Journal* vol. 4 no. 3–4 (July-Oct. 1978).

33. Eichengreen, *Toward a New International Financial Architecture*, p. 116.

34. 'The myth of the powerless state', *Economist*, 7 Oct. 1995.

35. Paul Krugman, *New York Times*, 2 Jan. 2000.

36. 'Challenge of globalization', *Financial Times*, 28 Dec. 1999.

37. Robert Kuttner, 'Economic viewpoint: The Seattle protesters got it right', *Business Week*, 20 Dec. 1999.

38. Dani Rodrik, 'Wereldhandel mag geen doel op zichzelf zijn', *NRC Handelsblad*, 8 Dec. 1999.

39. Eric Toussaint, *Your Money or Your Life!: The Tyranny of Global Finance*, London: Pluto Press, 1998, pp. 253–54.

40. See, for example, G. Albo, 'A world market of opportunities?: Capitalist obstacles and left economic policy', in Leo Panitch ed., *Socialist Register 1997: Ruthless Criticism of All that Exists*, London: Merlin Press, 1997; Elmar Altvater, *The Future of the Market: An Essay on the Regulation of Money and Nature after the Collapse of 'Actually Existing Socialism'*, London: Verso,

1993; Amin, 'De nieuwe wereldoverheersing'; Bernard Cassen, 'Impérative transition vers une société du temps libéré', *Le Monde Diplomatique*, July 1994; John Cavanagh, Daphne Wysham & Marcos Arruda, *Beyond Bretton Woods: Alternatives to the Global Economic Order*, London: Pluto Press, 1994; Ulrich Duchrow, *Alternatives to Global Capitalism: Drawn from Biblical History, Designed for Political Action*, Utrecht: International Books, 1995; Ewald Engelen, *De mythe van de markt: Waarheid en leugen in de economie*, Amsterdam: Het Spinhuis, 1995; Fourth International, 'Dictatorship of the proletariat and socialist democracy', *International Viewpoint* special issue: *Resolutions of the Twelfth World Congress of the Fourth International*, 1985; S. Halimi, Jonathan Michie & S. Milne, 'The Mitterand experience', in Jonathan Michie & John Grieve Smith eds, *Unemployment in Europe*, London: Academic Press, 1994; Michel Husson, 'Face à la contrainte extérieure', in *Agir ensemble contre le chômage: Données et arguments*, Paris: Syllepse, 1994; Kassa, *Nederland in spagaat: Pleidooi voor een andere ekonomiese logika*, Amsterdam: ISP, 1994; Tim Lang & Colin Hines, *The New Protectionism: Protecting the Future against Free Trade*, London: Earthscan, 1993; Ernest Mandel, *Long Waves of Capitalist Development: A Marxist Interpretation*, London: Verso, 1995; Mandel, *Power and Money*, London: Verso, 1992; Richard Norman, *Free and Equal: A Philosophical Examination of Political Values*, Oxford: Oxford University Press, 1987; Richard Peet, *Global Capitalism: Theories of Societal Development*, London: Routledge, 1991; Tony Smith, *Lean Production: A Capitalist Utopia?*, Amsterdam: IIRE, 1994; Toussaint, *Your Money or Your Life!*; and Toussaint & Peter Drucker eds, *IMF/World Bank/WTO: The Free-Market Fiasco*, Amsterdam: IIRE, 1995.

41. See Toussaint & Drucker, *IMF/World Bank/WTO*.

42. For an account of the irreconcilability of economics and ecology under capitalism, see, for example, Duchrow, *Alternatives to Global Capitalism*, and Altvater, *The Future of the Market*.

43. See Smith, *Lean Production*.

44. On a relationship between plan, market and democracy that would be an alternative to both capitalism and the old bureaucratically-planned economies in Eastern Europe and the Soviet Union, see Altvater, *The Future of the Market*, pp. 237–62; Mandel, *Power and Money*; Catherine Samary, *Plan, Market and Democracy: The Experience of the So-Called Socialist Countries*, Amsterdam: IIRE, 1988; and Samary, 'Mandel's views on the transition to socialism', in Gilbert Achcar ed., *The Marxism of Ernest Mandel*, London: Verso, 2000.

45. '21st Century capitalism: How nations and industries will compete in the emerging global economy, part 2', *Business Week*, 19 Dec. 1994, p. 54.

46. See Kim Moody's outstanding book, *Workers in a Lean World: Unions in the International Economy*, London: Verso, 1997.

Bibliography

Achcar, Gilbert, *L'empire et l'argent: Essai sur les fondements de la stratégie impériale des Etats-Unis d'Amérique*, Paris: University of Paris VIII: Saint-Denis, 1993.

——, 'The strategic triad: The United States, Russia and China', *New Left Review* no. 228 (Mar./Apr. 1998).

—— ed., *The Marxism of Ernest Mandel*, London: Verso, 2000.

Agir ensemble contre le chômage: Données et arguments, Paris: Syllepse, 1994.

Altvater, Elmar, *The Future of the Market: An Essay on the Regulation of Money and Nature after the Collapse of 'Actually Existing Socialism'*, London: Verso, 1993.

—— & Birgit Mahnkopf, *Grenzen der Globaliserung*, Münster: Westfälisches Dampfboot, 1996.

Amin, Samir, 'De nieuwe wereldoverheersing van het kapitalisme: Problemen en vooruitzichten', *Vlaams Marxistisch Tijdschrift* vol. 28 no. 3 (1994).

Andreff, Wladimir, *Les multinationales globales*, Paris: La Découverte, 1996.

Andriessen, Jacobus & Rob van Esch, 'Globalisering: een zekere trend', *Discussienota* vol. 3 no. 1, The Hague: Ministerie van Economische Zaken, 1993.

Archibugi, Daniele & Jonathan Michie, 'The globalisation of technology: A new taxonomy', *Cambridge Journal of Economics* no. 19 (1995).

—— eds, *Technology, Globalisation and Economic Performance*, Cambridge: Cambridge University Press, 1997.

Baker, Dean et al., *Globalization and Progressive Economic Policy*, Cambridge: Cambridge University Press, 1998.

Bandzak, Ruth, 'The role of labor in post-socialist Hungary', *Journal of Economic Issues*, vol. 28 no. 2 (1994).

Bank for International Settlements (BIS), *64th Annual Report*, Basel: BIS, 1994.

Barnet, Richard & John Cavanagh, *Global Dreams: Imperial Corporations and the New World Order*, New York: Simon & Schuster, 1994.

Barsoc, Christian, *Les rouages du capitalisme: Eléments d'analyse économique marxiste*, Paris: La Brèche, 1994.

Bello, Walden, & Stephanie Rosenfeld, *Dragons in Distress: Asia's Miracle in Crisis*, San Francisco: Institute for Food and Development Policy, 1990.

Bensaïd, Daniel, *La discordance des temps: Essais sur les crises, les classes, l'histoire*, Paris: Editions de la Passion, 1995.

——, *Marx l'intempestif: Grandeurs et misères d'une aventure critique (XIXe-XXe siècles)*, Paris: Fayard, 1995.

Bolkestein, Frits, *Het heft in handen*, Amsterdam: Prometheus, 1995.

Bonefeld, Werner, Richard Gunn & Kosmo Psychopedis eds, *Open Marxism*, London: Pluto Press, 1992.

Bonefeld, Werner & John Holloway eds, *Global Capital, National States and the Politics of Money*, London: St Martin's Press, 1995.

Boot, Hans, 'Management-filosofieën – van school tot bedrijf: De tijd van onderschatting is voorbij', *Solidariteit* no. 68 (1995).

Boyer, Robert, *The Convergence Hypothesis Revisited: Globalization but Still the Century of Nations?*, Paris: CEPREMAP-CNRS-EHESS, 1993.

—— & Daniel Drache, *States against Markets*, London: Routledge, 1996.

—— & Jean-Pierre Durand, *L'après-fordisme*, Paris: Syros, 1998.

Brenner, Robert, 'The economics of global turbulence', *New Left Review* no. 229 (1998).

Cassen, Bernard, 'Impérative transition vers une société du temps libéré', *Le Monde Diplomatique*, July 1994.

——, 'Technologie? Connais pas', *Le Monde Diplomatique*, July 1994.

Cavanagh, John, Daphne Wysham & Marcos Arruda, *Beyond Bretton Woods: Alternatives to the Global Economic Order*, London: Pluto Press, 1994.

Chesnais, François, *La mondialisation du capital*, Paris: Syros, 1994.

——, 'Mondialisation du capital et régime d'accumulation à dominante financière', *Agones: Philosophie, Critique & Littérature* vol. 16 (1996).

——, *Tobin or not Tobin?: Une taxe internationale sur le capital*, Paris: L'Esprit Frappeur, 1999.

—— ed., *La mondialisation financière: Genèse, coût et enjeux*, Paris: Syros, 1996.

Clarke, Simon, *Keynesianism, Monetarism and the Crisis of the State*, Aldershot: Edward Elgar, 1988.

Commission of the European Communities, *Employment in Europe 1993*, Brussels: Commission of the European Communities, 1993.

Connolly, Bernard, *The Rotten Heart of Europe: The Dirty War for Europe's Money*, London: Faber & Faber, 1995.

Coutrot, Thomas, *L'entreprise néo-liberale: Nouvelle utopie capitaliste?*, Paris: La Découverte, 1998.

Cuyvers, Ludo, 'Naar nieuwe internationale spelregels?', *Maandschrift Economie* no. 58 (1994).

Dicken, Peter, *Global Shift: Industrial Change in a Turbulent World*, London: Harper & Row, 1986.

Diwan, Ishac, & Ana Revenga, 'The outlook for workers in the 21st century', *Finance and Development*, Sept. 1995.

Doremus, Paul et al., *The Myth of the Global Corporation*, Princeton: Princeton University Press, 1998.

Duchrow, Ulrich *Alternatives to Global Capitalism: Drawn from Biblical History, Designed for Political Action*, Utrecht: International Books, 1995.

Duggan, Penelope & Heather Dashner eds, *Women's Lives in the New Global Economy*, Amsterdam: IIRE, 1994.

Eichengreen, Barry, *Toward a New International Financial Architecture: A Practical Post-Asia Agenda*, Washington: Institute for International Economics, 1999.

Engbersen, Gottfried, Anton Hemerijck & Wieger Bakker, *Zorgen in het Europese huis: Verkenningen over de grenzen van nationale verzorgingsstaten*, Amsterdam: Boom, 1994.

Engelen, Ewald, *De mythe van de markt: Waarheid en leugen in de economie*, Amsterdam: Het Spinhuis, 1995.

Foley, Duncan, *Understanding Capital: Marx's Economic Theory*, Cambridge: Harvard University Press, 1986.

Fourth International, 'Dictatorship of the proletariat and socialist democracy', *International Viewpoint* special issue: *Resolutions of the Twelfth World Congress of the Fourth International*, 1985.

Freeman, Christopher, 'The economics of technical change', *Cambridge Journal of Economics* no. 18 (1994).

Fukuyama, Francis, *The End of History and the Last Man*, London: Penguin, 1992.

Goldstein, Joshua, *Long Cycles, Prosperity and War in the Modern Age*, New Haven: Yale University Press, 1988.

Gordon, David, 'The global economy: New edifice or crumbling foundations?', *New Left Review* no. 168 (Mar.-Apr. 1988).

Gough, Ian, 'Economic institutions and the satisfaction of human needs', *Journal of Economic Issues* vol. 28 no. 1 (1994).

Gowan, Peter, *The Globalization Gamble: The Dollar/Wall Street Regime and Its Consequences*, n.p., 1998.

Greider, William, *One World, Ready or Not: The Manic Logic of Global Capitalism*, New York: Simon & Schuster, 1997.

Harvey, David, *The Condition of Postmodernity*, Oxford: Basil Blackwell, 1990.

Helleiner, Eric, 'Explaining the globalization of financial markets: Bringing the states back in', *Review of International Political Economy* vol. 2 no. 2 (1995).

——, 'Freeing money: Why have states been more willing to liberalize capital controls than trade barriers?', *Policy Sciences* no. 27 (1994).

Henderson, David, *The Changing Fortunes of Economic Liberalism: Yesterday, Today and Tomorrow*, London: Institute of Economic Affairs, 1998.

Hirst, Paul & Graham Thompson, *Globalization in Question*, Cambridge: Polity Press, 1996.

Hobsbawm, Eric, *Age of Extremes: The Short Twentieth Century, 1914-1991*, London: Michael Joseph, 1994.

——, 'Guessing about global change', *International Labor and Working-Class History*, no. 47 (1995).

Husson, Michel, *Misère du capital: Une critique du néoliberalisme*, Paris: Syros, 1996.

Irwin, Douglas, 'The United States in a new global economy?: A century's perspective', *American Economic Review* vol. 86 no. 2 (1996).

Kalshoven, Frank, *Over marxistische economie in Nederland, 1883-1939*, Amsterdam: Thesis Publishers, 1993.

Kassa, *Nederland in spagaat: Pleidooi voor een andere ekonomiese logika*, Amsterdam: ISP, 1994.

Kébabdjian, Gérard, *L'économie mondiale: Enjeux nouveaux, nouvelles théories*, Paris: Editions du Seuil, 1994.

Klein, Philip, 'A reassessment of institutionalist-mainstream relations', *Journal of Economic Issues* vol. 28 no. 1 (1994).

Kleinknecht, Alfred, *Heeft Nederland een loongolf nodig?: Een neo-Schumpeteriaans verhaal over bedrijfswinsten, werkelegenheid en export*, Amsterdam: VU, 1994.

—— & Jan ter Wengel, 'Feiten over globalisering', *Economisch Statische Breichten*, 6 Oct. 1996.

——, Ernest Mandel & Immanuel Wallerstein eds, *New Findings in Long-Wave Research*, New York: St Martin's Press, 1992

Koechlin, Tim, 'A critical assessment of the debate over Nafta', *Review of Radical Political Economics* vol. 25 no. 3 (1993).

Krueger, Anne, 'Trade policy and economic development: How we learn', *American Economic Review* vol. 87 no. 1 (1997).

Krugman, Paul, *The Return of Depression Economics*, New York: W.W. Norton, 1999.

Krumm K. et al., 'Transfers and the transition from central planning', *Finance & Development*, Sept. 1995.

Lang, Tim & Colin Hines, *The New Protectionism: Protecting the Future against Free Trade*, London: Earthscan, 1993.

Levy-Livermore, Amnon, *Handbook on the Globalization of the World Economy*, Cheltenham: Edward Elgar, 1998.

Liêm, Hoang Ngoc, *Salaires et emploi: Une critique de la pensée unique*, Paris: Syros, 1996.

Longworth, Richard, *Global Squeeze: The Coming Crisis for First-World Nations*, Lincolnwood: Contemporary Books, 1998.

Mandel, Ernest, *Introduction to Marxist Economic Theory*, New York: Pathfinder, 1970.

——, *Late Capitalism*, London: Verso, 1978.

——, *Long Waves of Capitalist Development: A Marxist Interpretation*, London: Verso, 1995 [earlier edition: *Long Waves of Capitalist Development: The Marxist Interpretation*, Cambridge: Cambridge University Press, 1980].

——, *Power and Money*, London: Verso, 1992.

——, *The Second Slump: A Marxist Analysis of Recession in the Seventies*, London: NLB, 1978.

Marglin, Stephan, & Juliet Schor eds, *The Golden Age of Capitalism: Reinterpreting the Postwar Experience*, Oxford: Clarendon Press, 1991.

Marx, Karl, *Capital*, vol. 3, Harmondsworth: Penguin, 1981.

May, Ann & Kurt Stephenson, 'Women and the great retrenchment: The political economy of gender in the 1980s', *Journal of Economic Issues* vol. 28 no. 2 (1994).

Meiksins Wood, Ellen, '"Globalization" or "globaloney"', *Monthly Review*, Feb. 1997.

Mensink, Nico and Peter van Bergeijk, 'Globlablablah', *Economisch Statistische Berichten*, 6 Nov. 1966.

Michelet, Charles-Albert, *Le capitalisme mondial*, Paris: Quadrige/PUF, 1998.

Michie, Jonathan & John Grieve Smith eds, *Employment and Economic Performance: Jobs, Inflation, and Growth*, Oxford: Oxford University Press, 1997.

——, *Managing the Global Economy*, Oxford: Oxford University Press, 1995.

——, *Unemployment in Europe*, London: Academic Press, 1994.

Miliband, Ralph, *Socialism for a Sceptical Age*, Cambridge: Polity, 1994.

—— & Leo Panitch eds, *Socialist Register 1992: New World Order?*, London: Merlin Press, 1992.

——, *Socialist Register 1993: Real Problems, False Solutions*, London: Merlin Press, 1993.

——, *Socialist Register 1994: Between Globalism and Nationalism*, London: Merlin Press, 1994.

Millman, G., *The Vandals' Crown: How Rebel Currency Traders Overthrew the World's Central Banks*, New York: Free Press, 1995.

Mishel, Lawrence, Jared Bernstein & John Schmitt, *The State of Working America 1998-99*, Ithaca: Cornell University Press, 1999.

Montes, Pedro, *El desorden neoliberal*, Madrid: Editorial Trotta, 1996.

Moody, Kim, 'Theses on the new GATT and the future of imperialism', *Solidarity Pre-Convention Bulletin* no. 6 (1994).

——, *Workers in a Lean World: Unions in the International Economy*, London: Verso, 1997.

Moseley, Fred, & Martha Campbell eds, *New Investigations of Marx's Method*, Highland Park: Humanities Press, 1997.

Murray, Robin, 'The internationalization of capital and the nation state', *New Left Review* no. 67 (1971).

Nader, Ralph et al., *The Case Against Free Trade: GATT, NAFTA, and the Globalization of Corporate Power*, San Francisco: Earth Island, 1993.

Naím, Moisés, 'Latin America the morning after', *Foreign Affairs*, July-Aug. 1995.

Nierop, Tom, 'De opkomst van de "Trillion-dollar-mega-netwerks"', *Business Topics* vol. 2 no. 1 (1995).

Norman, Richard, *Free and Equal: A Philosophical Examination of Political Values*, Oxford: Oxford University Press, 1987.

O'Hara, Phillip, 'An institutionalist review of long wave theories: Schumpeterian innovation modes of regulation and social structures of accumulation', *Journal of Economic Issues* vol. 28 no. 2 (1994).

Ohmae, Kenneth, *The End of the Nation State*, New York: Free Press, 1995.

Oman, Charles, 'Technological change, globalisation of production and the role of multinationals', *Innovations: Cahiers d'économie de l'innovation* vol. 5 (1997).

Ormerod, Paul, *The Death of Economics*, London: Faber and Faber, 1994.

Overbeek, Henk, 'Mondialisering en regionalisering: De wording van een Europese migratiepolitiek', *Migrantenstudies* no. 2 (1994).

—— ed., *Restructuring Hegemony in the Global Political Economy: The Rise of Transnational Neo-Liberalism in the 1980s*, London: Routledge, 1993.

Panitch, Leo, ed., *Socialist Register 1997: Ruthless Criticism of All that Exists*, London: Merlin Press, 1997.

Partido Socialista de los Trabajadores (PST), *Proyecto de Resolución sobre la Coyuntura Nacional*, Montevideo: PST, 1995.

Peet, Richard, *Global Capitalism: Theories of Societal Development*, London: Routledge, 1991.

Petrella, Ricardo, 'Les nouvelles Tables de la Loi', *Le Monde Diplomatique*, Oct. 1995.

Piot, Olivier, *Finance et économie: La fracture*, Paris: Le Monde-Editions, 1995.

Pritchett, Lant, 'Forget convergence: Divergence past, present and future', *Finance & Development*, June 1995.

Reich, Robert, *The Work of Nations*, New York: Vintage Books, 1992.

Renzi, Maria, 'Globalization and adjustment policies in Central America', *LOLA Press* no. 9 (Nov. 1995–Mar. 1996).

Reuten, Geert, 'Accumulation of capital and the foundation of the tendency of the rate of profit to fall', *Cambridge Journal of Economics* vol. 15 (1991).

—— & Michael Williams, *Value-Form and the State: The Tendencies of Accumulation and the Determination of Economic Policy in Capitalist Society*, London: Routledge, 1989.

Rodrik, Dani, *Has Globalization Gone Too Far?*, Washington: Institute for International Economics, 1997.

——, *The New Global Economy and Developing Countries: Making Openness Work*, Washington: Johns Hopkins University Press, 1999.

Roe Smith, Merritt & Leo Marx eds, *Does Technology Drive History?: The Dilemma of Technological Determinism*, Cambridge: MIT Press, 1995.

Ross, John, *Rebellion from the Roots: Indian Uprising in Chiapas*, Monroe: Common Courage Press, 1995.

Rudolph, Hedwig & Mirjana Morokvasic eds, *Bridging States and Markets: International Migration in the Early 1990s*, Berlin: Sigma, 1993.

Ruigrok, Winfried & Rob van Tulder, *The Logic of International Restructuring*, London: Routledge, 1995.

——, 'Misverstand globalisering', *Economisch Statistische Berichten*, 25 Dec. 1995.

Samary, Catherine, *Plan, Market and Democracy: The Experience of the So-Called Socialist Countries*, Amsterdam: IIRE, 1988.

Sassen, Saskia, *The Global City: New York, London, Tokyo*, Princeton: Princeton University Press, 1991.

——, *Losing Control: Sovereignty in an Age of Globalization*, New York: Columbia University Press, 1996.

Schwab, Charles & Claude Smadja, 'Power and policy: The new economic world order', *Harvard Business Review*, Nov.–Dec. 1994.

Sebaï, Farida & Carlo Vercellone eds, *Ecole de la régulation et critique de la raison économique*, Paris: L'Harmattan, 1994.

Shutt, Harry, *The Trouble with Capitalism*, London: Zed Books, 1998.

Slot, Birgit & Laurens Meijaard, 'Het dictaat van de kapitaal-stromen', *Economisch Statistiche Berichten*, 31 Aug. 1994.

Smith, Tony, *Lean Production: A Capitalist Utopia?*, Amsterdam: IIRE, 1994.

Sociaal-Economische Raad, *Europa na Maastricht*, The Hague: SER, 1993.

Solomon, Steven, *The Confidence Game: How Unelected Central Bankers Are Governing the Changed World Economy*, New York: Simon & Schuster, 1995.

Soros, George, *The Crisis of Global Capitalism: Open Society Endangered*, Boston: Little, Brown, 1998.

Stubbs, Richard & Geoffrey Underhill eds, *Political Economy and the Changing Global Order*, Houndmills: MacMillan, 1994.

Tilly, Charles, 'Globalization threatens labor's rights', *International Labor and Working-Class History* no. 47 (1995).

Tobin, James, 'A proposal for international monetary reform', *Eastern Economic Journal* vol. 4 no. 3-4 (July-Oct. 1978).

Toussaint, Eric, *Your Money or Your Life!: The Tyranny of Global Finance*, London: Pluto Press, 1998.

—— & Peter Drucker eds, *IMF/World Bank/WTO: The Free-Market Fiasco*, Amsterdam: IIRE, 1995.

United Nations Conference on Trade and Development (UNCTAD), *Trade and Development Report 1997*, Geneva: UN, 1997.

——, *World Investment Report 1994: Transnational Corporations, Employment and the Workplace*, New York: UNCTAD, 1994.

——, *World Investment Report 1998: Trends and Determinants*, New York: UNCTAD, 1998.

United Nations Development Programme (UNDP), *Human Development Report 1998*, New York: Oxford University Press, 1998.

——, *Human Development Report 1999*, New York: Oxford University Press, 1999.

Van Bottenburg, Maarten, *'Aan de Arbeid!': In de wandelgangen van de Stichting van de Arbeid, 1945-1995*, Amsterdam: Bert Bakker, 1995.

Van Dam, Marcel, *De opmars der dingen*, Putten: Balans, 1994.

Van de Ven, A. & A. Kok, 'De toekomst van de industrie', *Economisch Statistische Berichten*, 23 Mar. 1994.

Van Duijn, Jaap, *De longe golf in de economie*, Assen: Van Gorcum, 1979.

Van Kersbergen, Kees, Paul Lucardie & Hans-Martien ten Napel eds, *Geloven in macht: De christen-democratie in Nederland*, Amsterdam: Het Spinhuis, 1993.

Van Paridon, Kees, 'Een relevantere handelsmaatstaf', *Economisch Statistische Berichten*, 6 Nov. 1966.

Van Staveren, Irene, *Economie: vrouwelijk; staathuiskunde. Econoom: mannelijk; staathuiskundige (Van Dale, 1976)*, Utrecht: Oikos, 1995.

Van Witteloostuijn, Arjen, *De anorexiastrategie: Over de gevolgen van saneren*, Amsterdam: De Arbeiderspers, 1999.

Vernon, Raymond, *In the Hurricane's Eye: The Troubled Prospects of Multinational Enterprises*, Cambridge: Harvard University Press, 1998.

Vogel, Steven, *Freer Markets, More Rules: Regulatory Reform in Advanced Industrial Countries*, Ithaca: Cornell University Press, 1996.

Wallerstein, Immanuel, 'Declining states, declining rights?', *International Labor and Working-Class History* no. 47 (1995).

Walter, Andrew, *World Power and World Money*, New York: Harvester Wheatsheaf, 1993.

Weiss, Linda, *The Myth of the Powerless State*, Ithaca: Cornell University Press, 1998.

Went, Robert, 'Game, set and match for Mr. Ricardo?: The surprising comeback of protectionism in the era of globalising free trade', *Journal of Economic Issues*, Forthcoming in Sept. 2000.

Wriston, Walter, 'Technology and sovereignty', *Foreign Affairs* vol. 67 no. 2 (1988).

Index